ABOUT FACE

The Life and Times of Dottie Ponedel:
Make-up Artist to the Stars

by
Dorothy Ponedel
& Meredith Ponedel

with Danny Miller

BearManor Media
2018

Published in the USA by:
BearManor Media
P O Box 71426
Albany, Georgia 31708
www.bearmanormedia.com

Printed in the United States of America
ISBN 978-1-62933-285-7 (paperback)

Book & cover design and layout by Darlene Swanson • www.van-garde.com

To all the past, present, and future
female make-up artists everywhere
who fought to break the glass ceiling.
You are the heart and soul of this industry.

Contents

Acknowledgments

From Meredith Pondel:

I would like to acknowledge the following people whose help over the years has made this dream possible:

Kate Russell—your unflagging support and superb wordsmanship (I just made that word up) made me realize that this could really happen.

James Zeruk, Jr.—researcher and encouragement-giver extraordinaire. Thank you for all the pushing!

Leslie Rugg—the title giver. So simple and yet so elegant—and perfect.

Ned Comstock at the USC Archives—you always knew it could be done—even when I wasn't too sure.

And last but not at all least—Charles Miller, for letting me borrow his dad so often. This final result would not have happened without him.

Over the years, I have been privileged to have been gifted with photos of Dot with her various clients. I would like to give thanks and credit to the following friends who have been so generous. In alphabetical order:

Ned Comstock

John Fricke

Randy Henderson

Charles Triplett

Marc Wanamaker

From Danny Miller:

It was thrilling to work on this manuscript and to learn about the talent, humor, and endearing personality of Dottie Ponedel, a true pioneer in movie history. Dottie deserves so much acclaim for not only creating some of the most stunning and iconic faces in classic movies, but also for being such a loyal and devoted friend and confidante to all the marvelously talented individuals with whom she came in contact.

I so enjoyed collaborating with Meredith Ponedel, a superb keeper of the flame of her family's important legacy and whose childhood friendships with people like Judy Garland and Joan Blondell and her curiosity about her aunt's collection of old photographs and clippings got the ball rolling on this book so many years ago. I am grateful to the members of the Going to the TCM Festival Facebook group for bringing Meredith to our annual gathering in Hollywood where I heard about her Aunt Dot for the first time.

Meredith and I both thank Ben Ohmart and BearManor Media for helping us bring Dottie's story to the world. I've never seen a book from BearManor Media that I didn't want to devour from cover to cover so it's great to be a part of their wonderful booklist.

I want to thank my mother, another Judy, for introducing me to so many of the great films of the 1930s and 40s when I was a kid. And a special thanks to my wife, Kendall Hailey, whose knowledge of the golden age of movies is surpassed only by her brilliant writing and editing skills.

Finally, I thank Dottie Ponedel for allowing me to get to know her through her amazing, funny, and heartwarming stories.

147 N. Willaman Drive
Beverly Hills, Calif.
February 23, 1942

Make-Up Artists Local Union #706,
1627 N. Cahuenga Ave.
Hollywood, Calif.

Attention: Mr. E. Westmoore.

Gentlemen:

Again I have been informed that there is a movement to oust me from the Union for the crime of being a Woman. This certainly is not in keeping with the ideals and purposes for which the unions have been formed and operated.

For thirteen years I have been employed in this work, and for a like number of years I have been a member in good standing, and have paid my regular dues to the Union. That my work has been of the very highest calibre can be attested by the fact that I have always worked for salaries above the minimum scale, and that many of the leading stars have had clauses inserted in their contracts insisting upon my services. However, not withstanding this, I have at all times insisted that a make-up man be employed on any set where I have worked, as well as a body make-up girl where there was any of that work to be done.

My conduct, my workmanship, and my reputation, both as a lady and an artist, is, and has always been above reproach and is a matter of record. In all my contacts I have acted in a manner that would reflect nothing but credit to the proffesion and the Union. My efforts have been untiring in making women make-up consious, especially so in the Moving Picture industry where my efforts are well known.

This is the second time this ouster movement has been instituted, and I am sure all fair minded members of the Union can see the un-fairness of the action. For thirteen years I have devoted my life to this art, with ability, enterprise, and diligence. The very base of our democratic type of government, the Bill Of Rights, grants every person the right to pursue gainful employment, and to stop me now would be to deprive me of my means of livelihood.

In all fairness, Gentlemen, and for the good of the Union and the Proffesion, I ask that this action be premenantly withdrawn, and permit me to earn a living peacefully.

Yours truly,

Dot Ponedel.

Though at the top of her craft, Dottie Ponedel had to fight discrimination throughout her career. Here is Dot's impassioned letter to the Make-up Artists Local 706 after yet another attempt to oust her from the ranks because of the simple fact that she was a woman. Ponedel broke ground for all the women who came after her.

Introduction

by Meredith Ponedel

It wasn't easy for a skinny five-year-old to push that heavy box down the hall. I somehow managed to get it off the shelf and onto the floor and was now tugging and pushing it across the hall carpet to my aunt's room.

"DOTTIE!" I called out between huffs and puffs.

"WHATEE?" came the expected reply.

"I'm bringing you a box!" I yelled out excitedly. I was getting closer to her room and realized I had to maneuver her walker out of the way so I could get the box in. As she struggled to pull herself up in bed, I saw her glance down at me and my "find." A slow smile crept across her face as she saw what I had. I opened the box and looked breathlessly at the gorgeous face that now beamed up at me.

"Dottie, Dottie!" I exclaimed. "Who is this?"

Her smile got even bigger as she looked down at me. "Well, I'll tell you," she said. "Let's see who you've got there." She only needed the briefest of glances to identify her old friend. "Oh, that's Carole Lombard."

I took the picture back from her and studied it for a moment, taking in the blondest of blonde hair, the shadows that identified the cheeks, the faintest trace of a smile on her perfectly formed lips, and the lone long curl of hair that hung down teasingly from behind her ear. Then it was on to the next one.

I pulled out picture after picture, each one more gorgeous than the last. Not only the faces, but the costumes, the hair, the jewelry. I had never seen pictures like this before. These were not snapshots; they had absolutely nothing in common with the family photographs I was used to seeing. These were large, luscious pieces of photographic paper that were heavy and light at the same time. They were smooth to the touch and yet the photographic detail was so fantastic that the complexions stood out in grainy detail. They were rich and vivid and alive in my hands.

Another moment of examination as I studied another blonde lady, this one decidedly different from the first. She was wearing men's clothes which I found completely intriguing. A white fedora angled steeply over one eye gave her a rather mystical look. Her chin rested in the palm of her hand and she looked as though she knew I was looking back at her. A lady in men's clothes—wow.

"Who's this, Dot?"

"That's Marlene Dietrich."

I picked up another photo.

"Who's this, Dot?"

"That's Helen Hayes."

This lady was not at all like the other two fireballs I had just been introduced to. Helen joined Marlene and Carole in the growing pile on the floor.

"Who's this, Dot?"

"That's Mae West."

Holy cow—what a lady! Dressed in a gown with circles of white fur draped from her neck to her waist, with the remainder of the shimmering cloth arranged in a swirling pattern down to the floor and then another grand circle of white fur, this amazing person was leaning carelessly against a bannister staring straight at me and just daring me to say something. I was flabbergasted! Not as "nice" as the other ladies, I decided, but definitely interesting. I put her down and went for the next one.

"Who's this, Dot?"

"That's Paulette Goddard."

Everything about this lady was as fresh as a daisy in May. Her skin, her beautiful smile, the wide-brimmed straw hat she wore, the scarf tied jauntily around her neck—I decided that I really liked her!

"Who's this, Dot?" Again and again, all through the afternoon, I asked my aunt the same question. And again and again, she responded. More Lombard and Dietrich. More West and Goddard. Colbert, Gable, Cooper, Clara Bow, Maurice Chevalier, Lillian Roth, Henry Fonda, Joan Blondell, Gilbert Roland, Gladys Swarthout, Gail Patrick, and, best of all, Judy Garland.

There were also pictures of Dot in this amazing collection. Dot on horseback, Dot in a hula costume. Dot as an Indian. Dot in all sorts of amazing outfits and circumstances. And Dot was also in a lot of the pictures with the pretty ladies. Some showed Dot standing over them as they sat at a mirrored table and Dot was putting stuff on their faces.

I pulled out a heavy wooden scrapbook from the box that was bursting with newspaper articles. Dot said they were stories about her and the ladies.

When I had seen all of the incredible items in the box, I was nearly speechless.

"But Dottie, who *are* these people?" I demanded. "How do you know them?"

She carefully lowered herself into a more comfortable position in her bed. "Put all the pictures back in the box nice and neat. Then I'll tell you."

Little did I know that she would spend the next 20 years telling me her story—and I would spend the same 20 years eagerly listening.

"I rolled in on the old Sante Fe."

No matter how many times she told it, she loved to start her story this way...

1.

"I Rolled in on the Old Santa Fe..."

Irolled in on the old Santa Fe in 1920, cross-country from Chicago. Landed in Los Angeles with my mother and no job. Three hundred dollars between the two of us in a land we knew nothing about.

First thing, we had to find a place to live. We started hunting and found a small apartment on Lake Street opposite Westlake Park. It was $37.50 a month, furnished.

The next thing was, where to get a job? I didn't know where to go or what to do but I stopped to talk with a milkman and he told me about a Van de Kamp's Bakery for sale opposite Westlake Park on Seventh Street. There were a couple of bids for it but I offered a hundred dollars more than they did—our whole savings—and I got it.

Van de Kamp's would do the baking and bring the baked goods into the store at six in the morning. Mother and I worked on consignment; the more we sold, the more money we made.

The bakery happened to be in a lucky spot, right next to the bus stop where people could run in, get some pies, cakes, cookies and what-have-you, and run out to catch the next bus. Well, my mother was in seventh heaven because making a buck was all she cared about. And talk about selling bread! All the big mucky-mucks who came from the east sat in Westlake Park to pass the time away and fed the pigeons and ducks—and that took a lot of bread!

Dottie's mother, Ann, in their Van de Kamp's Bakery in Westlake Park.

In those days, there was no smog in Los Angeles and the stars in the sky were as big as your fist. It seemed like you could reach up and pick one out of the sky. The air was perfumed with orange trees and lemons and every kind of fruit you could think of—even bean fields which were close by. I remember the time I drove up Wilshire Boulevard and dug up a couple of wild rosebushes and took them home to my own backyard. Nobody would say anything.

I found myself getting up at 5:30 in the morning to hit the bakery by six. It was wonderful walking through the park at that time of day. Everything was great as long as we could make a dollar.

One morning at about 7:30, I noticed that a bunch of trucks loaded with movie equipment were parked outside our little shop. Some of the men came in for donuts and one of them noticed me standing behind the counter. We started talking and he asked me if I wanted to make five bucks as an extra. All I had to do was walk back and forth in front of the camera. I agreed right away, asked my mother to mind the shop, and spent the rest of the day on a movie set, walking back and forth, just as the guy had said. From there, I went to an old, tumble-down shack in Hollywood which was the casting office. This shack supplied all the studios with extras. I started going there whenever I could and got a lot of work. We earned from five to seven-fifty a day.

One day, when I was in the shack collecting my pay for a day's work, I noticed a native girl from the islands. I started talking to her and she told me she was an expert at the hula. She said she could teach me if I had any rhythm.

Dottie dancing the hula in one of her early film appearances in the1920s.

I turned out to be the best dancer on the west coast! Director

Tod Browning was making a picture called *Under Two Flags* (1922) with Priscilla Dean. Well, I was hired as the knife dancer in the desert in that film! After that, everyone wanted me. Mabel Normand was a top star on the Mack Sennett lot and she was also his sweetheart. One night we were all working on a Mabel Normand picture and she was supposed to do a Mexican Hat Dance. I ended up doubling for her dancing, jumping in and out of this big Mexican hat. Of course, Mabel got the close-ups but my feet got a couple of close-ups, too. Everybody had such a wonderful time that day. We had so much to eat and drink, it was like a big fiesta. Later that night, Mabel and Mack had a huge fight in her dressing room. I really thought they were going to come to blows. Everybody pretended they didn't hear anything but it was plenty loud.

The next day, there was a big commotion on the lot. Nobody could find the film that was shot the night before. Mabel, to get even with Mack, broke into the cutting room and stole the film and stashed it in milk bottles. She put the bottles in a box on her windowsill so you could only see the tops of the bottles. Nobody would ever dream of looking for the missing film there.

They searched that studio from top to bottom. Finally, Mack said they'd have to shoot the scenes all over again. By that time, Mabel had quieted down and was pretty calm and realized what she had done. She called the prop man and confessed. She had just wanted to get even with Mack.

Mack Sennett studio was over in Edendale right across the street from Clara Kimball Young's studio which we would often visit. We had so much fun on the Sennett lot with the Mack Sennett Bathing Beauties and the Keystone Cops, Charlie Chaplin, Harry Langdon, Wally Beery, and many more I could name.

One of Dottie Ponedel's first head shots from the early
1920s as she was starting out in the movies.

I remember the time I was tied to a railroad track and the train was supposed to go over me but never touched me. I used to jump off barns into haystacks and they would run the hand cars all over the lot with the Keystone Cops after us.

At that time, Carole Lombard was one of the Mack Sennett Bathing Beauties. Gloria Swanson was there and Ben Turpin who could cross his eyes any time and Snuff Pollard who was one of the Keystone Cops who would run around with his pants hanging down. This was about the time that Carole Lombard had a bad automobile accident. Years later, I made her face up for the camera at Paramount Studios. Carole was noted for that high forehead of hers and I never tried to change it like I did for other stars that needed it. The scar that went from her left nostril into her cheek was never noticed because I would fill it before I made her up.

Soon there wasn't a star in Hollywood that I didn't double for in dancing. I did every country, folk dance, Egyptian dance—any dance you can think of, I did. And the funny part of it was, except for my brief hula training, I never had a lesson in my life. And I always got an extra check from the director and the casting office for having the fire that it took to please the camera.

I remember doing a Spanish dance for the Greta Garbo movie *Torrent* (1926), and every colored flower that was in the Spanish shawl I was wearing was printed on my skin from the sweat! They had me dancing all day until Lew Cody, if you remember him, said, "Give that girl a rest before she falls on her face." That didn't mean a thing to me because I knew I was going to get an extra check for being such a good fake. With most of the dances I did, I never knew what my feet were going to do exactly, but it always came out great. And if they ever asked me to do it again, I could never do the same thing since I didn't really know what I was doing.

Dottie doing one of her specialty dances
in the early 1920s.

I remember back then I had a big REO car and I used to pick up five or six of us and go from studio to studio. Gilbert Roland was one of the gang. When we would hit the old Lasky Studios on Vine Street, I would see Mervyn LeRoy looking for extra work there, too, and, of course, he later became one of the giants of our industry. Gilbert Roland sure made it, too, because the women stars were crazy about him.

I remember once at the old Thomas Ince Studio, they had a black band and a white one. They had been rehearsing with a dance for several days with those two bands but the director wasn't satisfied with the dancer so he told his assistant, "Get me Dottie Ponedel!" When I heard this, I was worried that I wouldn't measure up but Danny, the assistant, assured me of getting a nice bit of money if I did. When I got there and into the costume and out on the set, I was scared out of my wits. And when they asked me which band I wanted, I said, "Let both bands double their time and play as loud as they can go 'cause I don't know where I'm gonna land!"

As soon as the take was done, the director yelled to Danny, "Why didn't you get me this ball of fire in the first place?" He came down and thanked me and asked me if I would like to have dinner with him. I knew what that meant and my knees started to hit each other. I felt something warm trickle down my leg. I looked down at the floor and behold! I had done it. I rushed to take the costume off and Danny put me in a limousine and sent me home because the assistant directors who knew me knew I was a good girl, but the directors didn't. After doing those dances, they thought I was a sure pushover but I wasn't.

I remember working with Rudolph Valentino on *The Four Horsemen of the Apocalypse* (1921). At that time, he was married to a little girl who played extra with us. Her name was Jean Acker. That was his first wife and she was just full of fun. When they got a divorce, Jean would always say, "I was his first wife, he was my first husband, and nobody can take that away from me."

I also worked with Valentino on *The Sheik* (1921). Vilma Banky was his leading lady then. She was a very beautiful girl. That picture was done on the old Lasky lot which was later Paramount Studios. We had about two weeks' work on that picture as they used a lot of extras. That was about the time that Jesse Lasky imported Pola Negri from Europe. He ordered a big shindig in her honor and told everybody they had to be there in full dress. He had two bands playing. It was the biggest party Hollywood had ever seen and at that time Gloria Swanson was the pet of the lot. Everybody catered to her and when she was told to appear at this dinner for this big foreign star, it didn't go so good with her and she never appeared. But with the entertainment and the good food, I don't think anybody missed her. I could see those love glances between Valentino and Negri, I knew something was going to happen there. They became buddy-buddy because they were always seen together. In *The Four Horsemen*, his leading lady was Alice Terry. Now Alice Terry and Rex Ingram, the director of the picture, were married. Rex Ingram was tall, handsome, and he should have been a star in his own right.

I even did a dance on a table once for D.W. Griffith, doubling for Lupe Velez, who later committed suicide. Yeah, I know what you're thinking—what am I, 101 years old? I'm going to say what all the other stars say: "I started at the age of two!"

Lou Tellegen was a European actor they brought to the old Vitagraph studio from Paris. He was Sarah Bernhardt's leading man. I was doing an Egyptian dance in that picture and after the picture he gave a big party in his Beverly Hills home. He asked Paul, a mutual friend of ours who was a Frenchman, to bring me up to this party. When we got there, everybody was loaded and when Lou saw me he saw the Egyptian dancer instead of the human being. I never ran up and down so many stairs in my life. I finally got outside and into Paul's car and laid down on the floor so I wouldn't be noticed when he came running outside. When Paul came outside I went "psst" and Paul came to the car and drove me home. He knew what was on Lou's mind. It seems every time I did a dance I got into trouble with the male sex.

Lou Tellegan was a Dutch-born silent film actor, screenwriter, and director
who made his film debut in 1911 opposite Sarah Bernhardt.

I remember I got a call to go up to the office of some honcho
whose name I forget—I think his first name was Abe. I thought I was
going to get a contract and I never moved so fast in my life. When I got
up there, he asked me so many questions about my life. I said, "What
has this got to do with what you want me for?" He said, "How would
you like to have a pretty house in Beverly Hills, pretty clothes, and
anything you want?" Well, I said to myself, here we go again. These big
guys had offices that looked like Grand Central Station. I did a hop,

skip, and jump around the oval table and he after me. Well, it got so funny to me I sat down and laughed out loud, even though I knew it was becoming serious because I could see that wild look in his eye. I told him everything he wanted to hear until I got out of that door.

My friend the native girl was called in for an interview at MGM and she asked me to come along. Lo and behold, I was picked for the part that she was hoping to do! They liked what I did so much that the next day, a director by the name of Hopper called me up and asked me to come down to the still department to pose for some pictures. Clarence Bull, the head of the still department, had a corner all fixed up with a couch, pillows, and drapes. Everything was ready. Hopper came in and said, "Now, Dottie, I want you to go in the dressing room and undress. We're going to take some nude pictures."

I turned around, gave him one look and said, "You must be kidding!" I told him, "I want all my interesting points draped or no go." I talked high, wide, and handsome and wound up posing for fancy bathing suits and knit suits published in the magazine under the MGM banner. The articles said that I had deserted the musical comedy stage to appear in their pictures which was the laugh of the century since my only previous job was working in the Boston Store in Chicago.

Dottie's early bathing suit photo that appeared in various magazines.

11

Ralph McCullough, Bob Custer, and Dottie Ponedel
in *Galloping Vengeance* (1925).

Ponedel as Little Wolf on her very first horse with Bob Custer as Tom Hardy
in *Galloping Vengeance* (1925).

I played an Indian character called Little Wolf in a film called *Galloping Vengeance* (1925) with cowboy star Bob Custer. Although I had a pear-shaped bust that pointed up to your nose, they tied those things down, put a dirty shirt on me, a dirty half-cut wig, a pair of lousy pants, and I was Little Wolf. We did our work in an old barn on Sunset Boulevard. Growing up where I did in Chicago, I don't think I ever even saw a horse but they plopped me on a horse that I thought was as big as a mountain. They asked me if I could ride and I said, "Oh, sure!" even though I was turning into stone from fright. I held onto the reins as the horse went up a steep hill. Bob Custer was right behind me on his own horse. As we looked down, we looked into kind of a small lake. After the shot was completed, I was so relieved as we were riding down the hill that I lost my balance and fell into the water! Believe it or not, whatever this water had in it, my hair was curly from then on. I told that story to Joan Blondell years later and she said, "Well, for God's sake, find out where the hell it is and let's go there!" I couldn't tell her where it was or where the location was 'cause I didn't know. Wished I did—I'd make myself a nice mint of money!

And believe it or not, my hair is still curly!

For several years I went on working—as a double for the stars, an Italian dancer at Universal, a French dancer at Warner Brothers, you name it, I did it. I remember when Carl Laemmle had Billy Wilder and Irving Thalberg at Universal. I believe that Billy was just a messenger boy then, while Thalberg was known as "The Genius" even though he was very young. Later on, Billy would direct these short westerns with "Hoot" Gibson and Art Acord. And if a company ever needed to go on location, the boss, Carl Laemmle, would say, "A tree is a tree and a stone is a stone. Do it on the back lot." There were no runaway pictures then for we all worked as a big family. Not only Universal but every studio in town.

13

Dottie played another Indian character, Annona Wetona, in
Border Justice (1925) with Bill Cody, Nola Luxford, and
Native American actor Tote Du Crow as her father.

Dottie (left) dances in *Across the Pacific* (1926) starring
Monte Blue and a young Myrna Loy.

Los Angeles was a very different town back then. I remember the night in the early 1920s when all of Los Angeles went downtown to Broadway to see the first streetlights lit up. The street dance that followed was a thing you would never forget because everybody you looked at seemed to be loaded. And everybody was making love to somebody. Too bad it couldn't go on forever.

After the streetlight dance, I got myself home as I had an early call the next morning at Universal. I was playing a gypsy girl, dancing on the streets of New York and banging on a tambourine, wearing some old dirty clothes that stunk to high heaven.

Dottie hoisted into the air on the set of *The Isle of Forgotten Women* (1927) starring Conway Tearle, Gibson Gowland, and Dorothy Sebastian.

In order to get to Universal City back then, you had to drive over the Cahuenga Pass. It was so high and narrow that two cars couldn't pass safely at one time. One car had to hug the mountainside while the other got around it to come down, or go up. The whole pass was lined with tall eucalyptus trees which filled the air with an aroma that was worth the trouble of getting up there. Universal often kept a bus waiting at the bottom of the hill to pick up the extras that couldn't make it up on their own. Today, you can drive over the Cahuenga Pass like any other street because the beautiful hill has been blasted away.

Not only was the Cahuenga Pass blasted away but Angels Flight, which was my favorite ride, has been disassembled. Angels Flight consisted of a small cable car, about half the size of the cable cars in San Francisco and about one third the size of the elevator that goes up and down the Eiffel Tower. The car started from Temple Street, went straight up a hill to a plateau which was called Bunker Hill. Sometimes, as I rode up and down, I would bring along a brown paper sack full of sandwiches and cookies. I would give the attendant some of these, hoping for a free ride. I usually got it.

I don't think there is anyone who loves Los Angeles more than I do and to see it cut up into a puzzle of freeways and our mountains blasted away and our beaches being polluted makes me really sad. What's happening to L.A.? They come and take your home away saying it's in the name of progress and they never even use the land they took from you and you're left without a home. I remember looking up at the mountains and the lights in the windows looked like glow-worms flittering all over the hill. What a beautiful sight! Now it's blanketed with a sheet of gray smog which damn near chokes you to death. Where is my beautiful L.A.? Her face may be marred but she's still called the City of the Angels.

One day, I was working on the Paramount lot, doing a hula dance and I overheard Charlie Boyle, the cameraman, discussing Nancy Carroll's make-up. He didn't like the spit-curls on her high cheekbones. Since she had a heart-shaped face, this made her cheekbones too prominent—Charlie was trying to make them less so. And me, with my big mouth, said, "Why don't you shade her face with a darker grease paint?" Nancy, who overheard me, asked me if I would try it out on her. I went to her dressing room and made her up in the way I thought she should be made up. Well, the test came out fine and Nancy went to the production office and asked if I could be put on the picture as her make-up artist. The production office said no, she couldn't have me. Nancy, with that Irish temper, said she'd do it herself. But she did such a lousy job—on purpose!—that the cameraman couldn't shoot it. They wasted a whole morning which would've paid my salary for a year.

Well, Nancy won a point because the production office called me the next day and asked me to come and make her up for the picture. The name of the picture was *Follow Thru* (1930), co-starring Buddy Rogers and Jack Haley.

It seems I had a natural talent for make-up and seeing how actresses or actors should look in front of a camera. From that time on, I did make-up only and was one of the first make-up artists under contract to Paramount. As the years went by, I stole whatever methods I could find, learned as much as I could from wherever I could, and perfected my make-up ideas and techniques.

I remember one time when I was working with Nancy Carroll, it was around Easter, and she asked me over for dinner. On the way to her house, I stopped and bought a live Easter bunny for her little girl who was around five years old. After dinner, she came to us and said she couldn't find her bunny. Nancy and I started to search the house. And guess where I found it—in the toilet, drowned. We all pretended to be searching for the rabbit while Nancy ran up to the pet shop and got another one. The little girl never knew anything about it. If she is reading this, it is the first time she will find out that she had a "stand-in" bunny!

At the studios, the make-up men hated my guts. They called me everything under the sun because I wouldn't make charts to show them what I was doing. Why should I, the way they were treating me? If they were smart, they would have done the same as I, take a little from this painting and that painting and use a little imagination and they would have the Ponedel make-up style. That's how I became so well known. A top dancer on the west coast, tops in my profession of make-up, with a lot of imagination, guts, and bluff. I became something the stars would yell for and I must say that the Man upstairs had his arms around me. I think he must like me a little bit as whatever I undertook to do, I always came out on top. Thank you, God.

2.

Marlene, Carole, and Paulette

Why is it the stars of today are nothing like the stars of yesterday? I'll tell you why. Because the studio would spend a half million dollars on a star they thought they could make a million on. The publicity alone would cost them a fortune. Then, perfect hairdos, make-up, gowns, and these stars would live up to what the studio wanted them to look like. The public got their money's worth when they saw these girls come upon the screen. Today, what we see on the screen is a bunch of jerks that all look alike, their hair stringy, jeans, sweaters, and if their bust isn't hanging over their waistline, they think they're not sexy. But to me, they look like hell. When we saw Crawford, Oberon, Dietrich, Garbo, Shearer, we knew we were going to see and get our money's worth because these dames really looked like stars.

In the early 1930s, I worked with so many great artists at Paramount. One of the best and most glamorous was Marlene Dietrich. Dietrich looked like any other person in *The Blue Angel* (1930), but when Joe Von Sternberg brought her back with him from a trip to Germany, the word glamour was introduced into our dictionary. Von Sternberg went to the front office and asked who had made up Nancy Carroll for *Follow Thru*. He wanted the same make-up artist to do a test for Dietrich the following day.

Dottie and Marlene Dietrich on the
Paramount lot in the early 1930s.

I think I had a hand in putting the most beautiful face on the screen and that was Dietrich. Every make-up artist in our industry wanted to know what I had done. Von Sternberg said, "Dottie, give her the works—give everybody something to talk about," and believe me, I did. I stole from the works of all the great artists—the Louvre had nothing on me. When all our stars at Paramount saw Dietrich on the screen, they all wanted to get that young, wide-eyed look. Believe me, Dietrich was really something to look at. I did things in the eye, around the eye, changed her hairline, and made a full, lush mouth. I added a subtle white line down the center of the nose which brought the nose up in case it had any inkling of being flat. I shaded the face when I wanted to get that hollow look. In order to do that, you had to get a lighter make-up in the center of the face and get a darker make-up toward the temples. Then, you'd take a light make-up over the lid of the eye and a darker grease toward the eyebrow which gives your eye a long full lid like Garbo. You know that would take you a good hour's work but the thing that scared the pants off of the stars was after they were done and powdered real well, I would take the pillows of my fingers, dip them in my rouge, and go over the skin of the face just where I wanted the pink color to come out. If you didn't know the touch of your fingers, you would spoil an hour or two's work but I knew just how far to go the minute my fingers hit the face. Now this was a wet rouge which would cake the whole make-up you had just worked on. Boy oh boy, when I got through they looked like a hand-painted picture and that was my secret of bringing luster to the camera. The stars would go to the front office crying they wanted Dottie on their picture. They wouldn't care how early they had to come in, as I could only do Marlene and a few of the top ones.

I remember the first time I went with Marlene to the still department to do some portraits. Travis Banton, head costume designer at Paramount, had just sewn Marlene into a black satin dress which fit skin tight. Marlene fell over a step she didn't see, right onto her belly. The dress split up the back and a full moon came into sight. I became hysterical because I had a perfect view, being about two feet behind her. Everyone burst out laughing, even Marlene, but when she saw that I was hysterical, Marlene got up and slapped me on both sides of my face. I then went into hiccups. They stopped but when I looked and saw her rear end sticking out, I started laughing all over again. Von Sternberg came in the studio to see how the portraits were coming along. The sight of Marlene's fanny sticking out didn't shock him a bit. He was used to seeing her walk around her dressing room in the nude.

A portrait of Marlene Dietrich inscribed "To Dot with my thanks for helping me to look beautiful."

Marlene would always sit in her dressing room at Paramount in the nude, chewing on tuberoses, but whenever anyone came through the door, I would throw a little colored pillow on her lap to cover up her thingamajig. Whoever it was, she'd say to them, "Look at Dottie, she's blushing for me!" Dietrich loved her figure and to her it meant nothing to be in the nude.

Dottie's close friendship with Marlene Dietrich lasted for the rest of her life.

I remember one afternoon, Marlene said to me, "Dottie, I'm going to pull a fake faint in front of Gary Cooper to see what it feels like to be in his arms without that goddamn camera ticking." Gary was about two feet behind us and as we opened the door to the set, Marlene fell to her feet. Gary grabbed her and held her. Nobody saw this but she winked at me as if to say, "Oh brother, this isn't half bad."

Dottie and Marlene on the set of one of her films in the mid-1930s.

That Christmas, Von Sternberg bought her seven diamond bracelets, each one half an inch thick. She almost dropped dead when she saw them because she had had a tough time in Germany during the war, having to eat beets about a hundred different ways. Even a cigarette was a luxury to her back then.

When she landed at Paramount, Marlene was the highest paid star in the industry. I remember one day Dietrich got into my Ford and there was a spring loose which jammed her good and she looked at me and said, "Dottie, we've got to do something about this." The following week there was a brand new Ford in my parking spot. It had everything in it but the kitchen sink. Frank Borzage and Gary Cooper walked me off the set and dangled the key in front of me as we got outside and Dietrich said, "I told you I'd do something about it." I was so shocked I started to cry and Dietrich said if she thought I was going to cry she wouldn't have bought it. But the presents didn't stop there. Marlene bought me a star ruby and many other presents and was also responsible for my getting a contract at Paramount. From the contract, I bought myself a pretty home in Beverly Hills.

I was a go-between for Von Sternberg and Dietrich every time they had a fight. There were two days she wouldn't eat because Von Sternberg would not talk to her and I climbed up the iron stairs to the cutting room where he was working and I said, "For God's sake, make up with Dietrich, she hasn't eaten for two days!" I started to cry. These were not crocodile tears, they were real, and Von Sternberg said, "I wonder if she knows what a friend she has in you." I don't think Sarah Bernhardt could have done any better on that crying scene than I did. That night, they had dinner and everything was sunshine and roses.

Dietrich would fix Von Sternberg's lunch every day in her dressing room because she didn't think the food in the commissary was good enough for him and during lunch no one was allowed to go near that door until Von Sternberg came out. As we all knew, there was plenty of hanky-panky going on but he was her Lord and Master at that time and he could do no wrong. He dominated every move she made and she would do nothing to hurt his feelings. That meant that when Von Sternberg was happy, we knew we were going to have a great day on the set. As long as the boss was flying high, we all followed.

I remember when a cousin of mine came out to Los Angeles from Chicago. I knew she had no money or clothes to speak of. I had to land her a job, but where? She was the type that men would turn around and look at twice. I explained this to Dietrich and she said, "What are you worried about? I'll make her my stand-in and that will get her $75 a week." Dietrich told me to make her up and she'd get Nellie Manley to put a blonde wig on her. Between Dietrich, Von Sternberg, and me, my cousin Pookie had a job. When she appeared on the set all made up like Dietrich, I don't think there was one guy in the troupe that didn't go for her. This was seventh heaven for Pookie, whose real name was Ruth. Dietrich and I got a big bang out of watching these guys make a play for her and of course, to Pookie, this was something that wasn't even real, but that's Dietrich—she will do anything to ease anybody's mind. She can get in a kitchen and make the best chicken soup and donuts you ever tasted and everybody in the industry knew about it, but I was the top guinea pig who got to sample everything she made. She would send a big platter of all these goodies home to my mother and, of course, the buttons on my mother's sweater would pop open to think that Dietrich would send the platters of goodies to her. Dietrich had a heart as big as all outdoors.

I did every picture Marlene made at Paramount, and had started working on some of the other stars. One morning, as I was making up Carole Lombard, she told me to put the white in her eye like I had

26

done to Dietrich. I put white liner on the shelf of her eye, which gave it a clear, young look but she grabbed the liner and put on a little more which made her eye go blurry and she could hardly find the set.

Dottie and Carole Lombard also had a very close friendship. She inscribed this portrait, "To Dottie Dear, Thank God for you. Otherwise, where would I be. Love and kisses, Carole"

While I was sitting there in Lombard's dressing room, the big boss came in and said, "Dottie, what do you think you could do with Mae West? She doesn't like the way she looks." My mind wasn't on Mae West just then. It was on a long string that Carole had just handed her older brother. She said, "Follow this string and what you find at the end of it is yours." The string went around the block of the studio and there, at the end of it, was a beautiful car. Her brother just about flipped his lid.

Carole was a great gal. Carole was noted for her swearing on the lot. She would dish out all those four-letter words and the crew loved it. We never knew whether Bill Wellman or Carole would dish out those words one after the other and when they did, they had to feed the kitty with money. Those four-letter words that came from Carole didn't seem dirty because she was always clowning with the electricians and prop men and believe me, they loved her. The crew on Lombard's pictures would be the happiest guys in the whole studio. She sure took care of them. She would always have donuts and coffee for them and in the afternoon she would have sandwiches and Coke brought in for the boys. Do you wonder why they loved her? She was a joy to be around. She was not a sourpuss—she loved to see her crew happy.

Carole liked a good prank, too. I remember years later, when she was married to Clark Gable, one morning Clark woke up and found an actual elephant in their front yard. As the elephant turned its rear end, he saw a sign that read, "Merry Christmas and Happy New Year, Clark!"

Carole loved children but never had the luck of producing one. Some people have luck and some don't, but I know how much Carole wanted a child with Clark, because she told me so. She wanted a baby so bad she tried everything but nothing happened. She told me once, "If I could have a baby every year, I would, whether the studio liked it or not."

Dottie was close to many of the children of her famous friends, including
Maria Sieber, Marlene Dietrich's young daughter who wrote "To Dot, Maria"
on this lovely portrait that Dottie kept in her make-up room.

In the 1930s and 40s, a star wasn't even allowed to be married or
say she had children. They had to sign an agreement to that effect
because the publicity would go out on them as being single so that

the public would have a terrific yen for them. But when Dietrich sent for her little girl, Maria, who was five years old, from Germany, she broke the ice for all our stars who were married and had children. She said the public will know we're human, whether the studio likes it or not.

Not having a child was a real sadness in Carole's short life. Do you remember the picture *Wuthering Heights* (1939) with Merle Oberon and Laurence Olivier when they walked hand in hand over the dunes into the night? Well, in my imagination, I always see Clark and Carole walking hand in hand over the hills and valleys of the City of the Angels. Oh, I could go on talking about Lombard forever but Mae West is waiting.

When I went to see Mae West, she looked at me and said, "Are you the gal who made up Dietrich and Carole and the rest on this lot?" I said, "Yes," and she said, "See what you can do with this face of mine." I had to do something fast—the whole front office was waiting for her.

Now I was up to my dirty work. I pulled out portraits and pictures by famous artists to see what I could steal from their paintings. Like the white in the eye, the plucked eyebrow, the gaunt look, the full lower lip, and many other little attractions I used.

I wound up going to Mae West's apartment every morning after I made up our regular stars. All the furniture in her apartment was white and in her bedroom was a mirrored ceiling with a big stuffed monkey hanging on the bedpost. This really intrigued me and I sure enjoyed those big hot breakfasts waiting for me every morning. You could have ham, hot buns, honey, you name it, you could have it. I couldn't wait from one morning to the next. Mae is one of the shrewdest women in Hollywood. I believe she still had the first greenback she ever made. She was never one to give presents or parties to anyone after a picture. Mae was out for Mae and what Mae wanted, Mae got. She was a shrewd businesswoman.

Mae West inscribed this photo
"To Dot, who makes me beautiful."

Dottie using her make-up tricks on the great Mae West.
Once West saw what Dottie could do, she insisted on
her services. "No stranger is going to pat this puss!"

Marlene was very different, in personality and in style. Dietrich looked as handsome in men's attire as she did in women's. She used to say, "If you feel beautiful inside, you will look beautiful on the outside." People talk about Dietrich being this and that but to me she was one in a million. Whoever needed a handout, Dietrich was there to give it to them. One day, we were looking at rushes in the theater from Marlene's latest picture with all the big shots at the studio. I'll never forget that day because Von Sternberg stood up at his seat and bawled the hell out of me in front of everybody. He said, "I don't want any more shading on Dietrich's face than you've already done. You just need to be more careful on the shading under the chin!" When the big shots left the theater, Dietrich said, "Why the hell did you bawl out the *Kleine* ("little one" in German) in front of everyone?" Von Sternberg came over to me and ran his hand through my hair. "I just want them to know how indispensable Dottie is so when her contract comes up and she asks for more money, they'll realize how important she really is with the stars on the lot." He raised my face up with his hand and said, "I didn't hurt your reputation, I added to it." Von Sternberg was a short man who always wore a beret and carried a cane. He was like a little Caesar on that lot. I've seen him put the heads of the studio off of his set and refuse to turn the camera on until they left. What he lacked in height he made up in stubbornness.

I remember when Marlene had her legs insured for a million dollars which makes me laugh when I think of those legs running up and down the lawn of her Beverly Hills mansion because her house guest, French actor Jean Gabin, had locked her out with no clothes on. She managed to climb in through a back window and into bed and covered up real warm. He was looking for her all over the grounds and couldn't find her. He became alarmed and he went back into the house and searched each room and finally found her in the bedroom under the covers.

That French actor had a physique that most women would go for. He was strong and sturdy and had a full head of blond hair. You could almost picture yourself making love to a guy like that. Dietrich looked up at him and said, "If I don't get pneumonia tonight, I never will," as her teeth were still chattering. He threw a hot toddy into her and you can imagine what happened that night.

Marlene was always so good to me. Anything I mentioned, she would send out and get for me. Half the time I was afraid to mention anything because if I did, it would be there in about an hour. One time, when I was sick and had the flu and couldn't come to the studio, she sent over six-foot-tall baskets full of flowers. There were 10 of them! The florist knew that Marlene did this for a joke but I would like to have had the money that joke cost her. I had all of those baskets sent to the Children's Hospital.

"Dot! As ever, Marlene Dietrich"

Dietrich had a heart of gold. If anyone got sick and she knew about it, she would get in her kitchen and cook a pot of chicken soup like you've never tasted before. She would fix donuts, coffee cakes, and she could make eggs 50 different ways. You talk about a gourmet cook—nobody had it on her. I remember one time when David Niven was sick and she heard about it, she ran over with a pot of hot chicken soup. She made up her mind she was going to get him well. Behind all that glamour was a real woman. I loved her dearly.

Dot's beloved house in Beverly Hills became a meeting place for many of her friends from the studio. She lived there until her death.

When I moved into my house in Beverly Hills, the housewarming that Dietrich gave me had I don't know how many cases of champagne with a zinnia flower stuck into each cork which made it look wild and picturesque. The window in the master bedroom went down to the floor which made it easy for anybody to jump out of. The crowd on the lawn hollered to Marlene when they saw her up there, "Come on and jump!" She started halfway through the window when I grabbed her by the seat of her pants and pulled her back. If she had broken a leg in the middle of a picture, they would have me sent to Siberia! The people who were yelling to her were Grace Bradley, Hopalong Cassidy's wife, Carole Lombard, Tallulah and Paulette, William LeBaron, a Paramount executive, and Kitty Kelly, LeBaron's sweetheart. I think anybody that was under contract at Paramount was out on my lawn yelling their heads off.

My house became a kind of halfway house for the stars of the 1930s. There was Clark Gable sizzling up some big steaks in my kitchen and flirting with Joan Blondell. Everyone loved to cook in my kitchen. People would smell the aroma of the cooking a block away but didn't know who was the chef at any moment. There was Carole Lombard with Russ Columbo just a week before the gun he was cleaning killed him. There was Gary Cooper with Countess Dorothy Di Frasso. I remember the Countess telling me that to have a home like this in New York, you'd have to be a millionaire.

I remember one evening, Countess Di Frasso called me and asked if I wanted to go to Pickfair as Mary Pickford was giving a big shindig. It was an honor to be invited up there so I went and when I got there, I saw Louella Parsons trying to put on some lipstick. She had half of it smeared on her chin and when she saw me she said, "Come on, Dottie, make me look pretty." I said, "I didn't come up here to work. I came up here to have some fun."

"Aw, come on, Dot, give me a hand!" And so I did. Dorothy Di Frasso was standing by and she saw Louella put two things in my pocket. They were rolled up tight into little balls—one dollar bills. I looked at it and laughed and so did Dorothy. I said, "Louella, you need this more than I do. You can't buy me that cheap."

"I must have made a mistake," Louella responded, but she hadn't. That was Louella. You couldn't invite Louella without Hedda as your name would be mud the next day in Hedda's column but I loved Hedda, because she was my good friend. There wasn't a week gone by that I wasn't in her column. Louella, on the other hand, would never give me a spread in her column. Somehow, she had no love for me. She favored the Westmore boys and I couldn't have cared less as there wasn't a columnist in our business that hadn't written about me from time to time.

Hedda was a great friend. I remember one morning I was working on Kitty Carlisle who was going to sing in a Paramount picture, and somebody knocked on the door and said, "I'm next." It was Hedda Hopper. As she sat in my chair she said, "Did you see the headlines about you in the paper this morning?" I said, "No, who did I kill?"

This was around the time that the Duke of Windsor was telling the world he was leaving the throne for the woman he loved. Paramount had to get their two cents in by saying that Dot Ponedel could take Wally Simpson and make her the most beautiful woman of our time.

> If Mrs. Wally Simpson were to choose an acting career, she could become a Hollywood star.
> This was the opinion voiced yesterday by Dot Ponedel, filmdom's most famous makeup woman, who declared that the reported fiancee of King Edward VIII has the necessary qualifications for success on the screen.

An excerpt from the article proclaiming that Ponedel could make a movie star out of Mrs. Simpson.

I said, "Hedda, that's news to me as I don't know what it's all about." The paper was full of it. It was a trick of the Paramount publicity department but oh boy, I think every studio in town was on the phone calling me. Hedda said, "Give me some extra make-up because I'm going up to the Hearst Ranch tonight. Everybody in the business will be there tonight."

I said, "Hedda, I would give half my life to see that place."

She said, "You know Marion Davies, don't you?" I said yes.

"Okay, Dottie, I'm going to call her and get you an invite." I said, "Don't do it—I have to be at the studio early Monday morning for all these stars or I'll get fired, contract or no contract." She said, "Just leave it to me."

Since it was only going to be for a weekend, I thought I could make it. Hedda called and said, "Grab an extra pair of slacks, you're going with us."

When the plane landed with all of us and we saw what we saw, it was like walking through a diamond with all its facets glittering. It was a sight that I don't think any of us will ever see again. This was like Shangri-La, the Taj Mahal, and the Vatican all in one.

The next morning, I was sitting in a corner on a stone bench all by myself when a great big carved wooden door opened and out walked William Randolph Hearst. He looked at me and put his arm on me and said, "Why aren't you with the rest of the crowd?"

After Mr. Hearst left, Hedda walked up and said, "Why have you been shaking your head for the past five minutes?"

I said, "Hedda, how did I climb so high? With all the stars and also in the presence of this great man, Mr. Hearst. Am I Cinderella or am I still the girl who was wrapping curtains in the department store basement?"

Hedda said, "Believe it or not, you're one of our celebrities and us gals all fight for you and some of us win. And if you don't get in a happier mood, I'm going to feed you to the elephants!"

Sometimes Gary Cooper would hide out in my house to avoid doing interviews or sitting for portraits at the studio. He always wound up talking about Dorothy Di Frasso when we were alone. He told me about her beautiful villa in Italy where she had glass floors with water running through them like a fountain. They were planning a hunting trip to Africa as Dorothy was a wonderful sharpshooter. I have some of the pictures they sent me, her with the lion and him with a couple of monkeys and when I first met Dorothy, I could read in her eyes the love the she had for that guy. Dorothy turned out to be my best friend because she knew I could transfer her thoughts to Gary and keep her happy with the nice things Gary would say about her. One day, a box came with olive green crêpe de Chine sheets, top and bottom, and pillowcases to match. On the pillowcases, the monogram was a foot high and a foot wide! I would also get large bottles of perfume. Dorothy would always send me something to keep me alive in her romance with Gary. This went on for some time until one party night when he met Rocky (Veronica Balfe) and before he knew it, he was engaged to be married. It happened so fast he didn't know it himself and, of course, that left Dorothy with a broken heart.

Dottie with Gary Cooper (left) and George Raft (right) on the set of
Souls at Sea (1937) where she was making up her friend Frances Dee.
Dottie wrote on the photo before sending it to a relative: "How do you
like my boyfriends? They do say hello."

We all looked out for each other back then. I remember sitting in Tallulah Bankhead's dressing room one day when the phone rang. They were trying to find me to tell me that my toy bull terrier had just been found dead. Of course, I started to cry because boy, I sure loved that dog. By that time Dietrich had heard about it and unbeknownst to Tallulah and Tallulah unbeknownst to Dietrich had each sent out for a variety of dogs. Two small vans came onto the lot with the animals. From Tallulah's group, I picked a white-haired terrier and from Dietrich's bunch, I picked a Pekingese—he damned near looked human. I got the two little animals home that night and started to put paper down all over the rugs as they were not housebroken. But, leave it to them, they would do their business where the paper wasn't.

"For Dot, with my love, from Tallulah"

Did I mention how I met Tallulah Bankhead? She had gone over to 20th Century Fox to do a picture. Ernst Lubitsch was to direct and he promised her that he'd arrange to borrow me from Paramount.

When she reported for work and got to the make-up department to look for me, she was told that I had died the month before! It turned out that the head of Fox's make-up department didn't want me around. Tallulah was shocked and immediately contacted Dietrich with the news. Dietrich just laughed and said, "Well, if Dottie died last month, who the hell made me up this morning?" They both had a good laugh over that.

Dottie and Marlene on the set of *Destry Rides Again* (1939) starring Dietrich and James Stewart.

Of course, it was Dietrich who introduced slack suits and pants for women in Hollywood. She used to have men's suits and trousers made for herself at Schmitz, where you couldn't get a pair of slacks for under $100, but her man's attire looked beautiful on her and that's how women started to wear pants. And today, women wear more pants than they do dresses, thanks to Dietrich.

Between Tallulah having these pretty slack suits made for me in exotic materials and Dietrich having her tailor make me up cute suits, I was the talk of the make-up union which was made up entirely of men. They didn't want to accept me into the union but they eventually had to take me because I was under contract. And stars like Marlene and Mae West fought for me, saying they wouldn't come to work unless I was accepted into the union.

Dottie chatting with Cary Grant on the Paramount lot in the 1930s. In addition to the women who she worked with, Dot became close friends with many of the male stars in the business.

We had a wonderful bunch of men on the Paramount lot. There was Cary Grant, Gary Cooper, George Raft, Buddy Rogers, George Bancroft, Richard Arlen, Dick Powell, Herbert Marshall, Melvyn Douglas, Bing Crosby, and Bob Hope. One day, George Raft came over to me and said, "I bet you two fox furs you can't get the information on my next contract." He knew that Bill LeBaron, a big executive at the studio, liked me an awful lot and that I could get information that they couldn't. When I came out, I said, "George, you're not only set for next year, but for a couple of years." The following week, George and his lady friend took a trip to New York, and guess what I got—two silver fox furs! When I put them around my neck I looked just like Smokey the Bear.

Around that time, Gary Cooper yelled over to me one day as I was walking past his dressing room. "Come over here, Dottie, I have a secret for you. De Mille has tested everybody that is anybody to do the French Indian girl in my picture and hasn't found anybody yet. Paulette Goddard would give her eyeteeth to get the part but she could not make the grade with him." I knew she'd be terrific in that part so I said, "All right, let's get her and I'll make her up and we'll get her dressed up right." When we got through with her, she looked terrific. It was lunchtime and De Mille was coming into his office from another test. Paulette sat on the corner of his desk as he opened the door, glared up at him and said, "I'm the girl you're looking for." He took one look at Paulette and said, "Cancel all the tests. Okay, Paulette, you got it." Paulette always had a case of champagne in her dressing room. By the time we finished the champagne, we both had a giggling jag on. Tallulah heard us and joined us and nobody loved champagne better than Tallulah. Pretty soon the whole gang was in Paulette's dressing room and Dietrich said, "What are we celebrating?" Paulette said, "I got the De Mille part thanks to Dottie!"

I managed to climb two flights of stairs to my make-up room and threw myself on the sofa. I could heard Paulette calling me from downstairs, "Dottie, Dottie, where are you?" But I was too loaded to answer. You can bet your bottom dollar I was on time the next morning since I never left my make-up room. I was still in my clothes, and I could still hear Paulette calling, "Dottie, Dottie."

Paulette Goddard called Dottie "Tinklebell" because of her distinctive laugh. She signed this photo, "To Tinklebell, whose kindness is as great as her artistry, with appreciation, Paulette"

I remember when Paulette Goddard and Charlie Chaplin had this pretty home in Beverly Hills. I was up there quite a bit. Paulette showed me her jewel box and I have never seen jewels like that in all my life and I have seen Countess Di Frasso's and Barbara Hutton's and I don't think any of them could compare with Paulette's. That is the smartest girl that ever drew breath. When she would have a date, it would only be with some man that was powerful or of big means. She would tell them not to bring her flowers or candy. "Bring me gems." I remember one time when one of our foreign directors sent her a sunflower made of real gems. That pin was up in the thousands. I remember Chaplin saying, "What was that that just came?" She said, "Oh, just some costume jewelry," and boy, then the fireworks started.

I recall when Robert Taylor and Barbara Stanwyck were married and so in love. It was her birthday. They were both working at MGM. Robert had arranged a surprise party that night which she knew nothing about. When they got home, Barbara said, "Let's take our showers, get comfortable, and get some rest before dinner." As she stood on the balcony of the stairway, she called over to him and said, "Bob, come on, let's have some yummy." "Yummy" was to Barbara and Bob what Eddie Cantor used to call "whoopee." Her guests, who were hidden in another part of the house, heard this and as Barbara stood on the balcony, they all came out and hollered, "Surprise!" It almost knocked Barbara off her feet as she wasn't dressed! The first thing they asked her was what was "yummy?" Barbara winked at Bob and said, "Yummy is a French dessert served on crackers, and is it good!" The crowd was never the wiser and they let it go at that. Those two sure made a beautiful couple. I know that Barbara did so much for charity, unbeknownst to the public. Especially for children's organizations. She was a big giver. She took after Sinatra that way.

Dottie worked with Barbara Stanwyck on several
films and the two became close friends.

Another guy I remember coming to Paramount was Maurice
Chevalier. I was walking with Dietrich one day when Chevalier
stopped us to chat for a minute. He looked at me and in that French
accent said, "You know, you look just like my wife," and he motioned
with his hand about the shape of his wife and me. In other words, he
was trying to say we were the same measurements. "She is coming today to have lunch at the studio and you will see what I mean." When
I met her there was quite a resemblance. I have a picture of Chevalier
and Eve. You would think it was me instead of his wife in the picture.

I have to laugh at a story he told me. "In America," he said, "I
always thought a man and a woman who slept together had to be
married. That's why I married Eve before I came here and when I
got here, I found out that there were more men and women sleeping
together that were not married than in all of France."

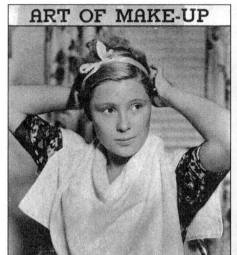

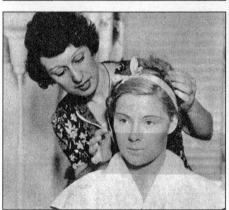

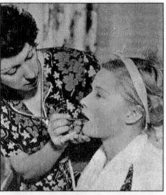

In the 1930s, many newspaper
and magazine articles profiled Dottie,
her friendships with the stars,
and her techniques for transforming
them into the great beauties of
the screen. This article featured
actress Mary Carlisle.

One of the portraits of Dottie used to advertise her expertise while she was at Paramount. Despite the acclaim Dottie received by everyone in the industry, the male make-up artists at the studio remained reluctant to accept a woman among their ranks.

When Eve went back to France, Chevalier stayed on to make two or three pictures with Paramount. He was lonely and asked me, "Dottie, do you think Marlene would have dinner with me some night?" He showed me a green emerald ring, which was about an inch long and an inch wide. The most beautiful gem I had ever seen.

I know Marlene could have had it if she had said yes, but when I asked her if she would have dinner with him, she said, "Dottie, every time I go out with a man they sit me in front of a fireplace, feed me cold chicken, and show me what a beautiful bedroom they have. Men are men the world over and Chevalier is no different. I don't want to hurt his feelings, Dottie, so you make an excuse for me." I told Chevalier that Dietrich was afraid of Von Sternberg and Chevalier said he understood.

I forgot to mention one guy I knew from the early days who was pretty special. He won the first Oscar for directing that was given in our industry for a picture called *Seventh Heaven* (1927) in which Janet Gaynor and Charles Farrell starred. His name was Frank Borzage. He was built like Spencer Tracy. I worked on that picture and I was secretly in love with this man. Every time he would come over and say, "Good morning, Dottie," I would just about melt away. I think he sensed that I had a little yen for him, that's why he was so nice to me. One time he put his arms around me and kissed me on the cheek and said, "Dottie, just stay the way you are and you won't get into trouble."

In later years, he came to Paramount and directed Gary Cooper and Dietrich and I told them how much I was in love with him many years before. Gary Cooper, who overheard the conversation, said, "Why didn't you nail him, Dottie"? I said, "I was too young back then and didn't know how to do it."

I still think of that man—he was so sweet to everybody and everybody loved him. He died at an early age. Every once in a while he comes before me, so he must have made a hell of a dent in my memory.

You know, when most of these men would look at me, they would have me undressed in their mind's eye and I didn't want to be sorry as to what would happen since there were no birth control pills in those days so I would always have a big fat excuse of saying no. I just didn't have the time to be worried about babies.

Sometimes the head of the studio, or a producer or director, would ask me to have dinner with them and I would say, "Look, what you want I haven't got." We would laugh and make a big joke about it. That's how I got away with it.

Oscar-winning actress Helen Hayes, also known as the "First Lady of the American Theatre" was thrilled to get Dottie's glamour treatment. She wrote, "To Dot, with love and gratitude" on this portrait.

Two other women I worked with at Paramount were Ruth Chatterton and Helen Hayes. Talk about the Taj Mahal being beautiful, I walked into Ruth Chatterton's bedroom and there was a canopy bed up on three tiers as you would walk up to a throne. It was done in pink satin. The windows were all around the room, covered with pink satin drapes. I thought I was walking into an ice cream cone. I looked at the bed and thought what could people do in that bed, but after all, she was married to Ralph Forbes who was a beautiful hunk of man and then I let my thoughts wander. She was on the phone talking to Helen Hayes who was coming over to the studio to do *The Sin of Madelon Claudet* (1931). Chatterton told Hayes to be sure to ask for Dottie when she arrived.

Helen Hayes was such a lady that I found myself tiptoeing into her dressing room every morning. Why, I don't know—but she was quite different from the girls I was used to making up. I could say all the four letter words with the other girls but I couldn't even say "damn" in front of Helen Hayes but I sure enjoyed working with her.

Ruth Chatterton never ate lunch. She always had a massage during her lunch hour. Many times I wished I could have laid down in her place and have that woman work me over, I was so pooped, but just being the hired help I just took what came naturally.

It wasn't easy for me in this business. Our make-up union was only made up of men, I was the only woman artist and they didn't like it one bit. Some of the guys there branded me as a lesbian. But having a mother like I had, I never knew the joy of a man until I was almost too old to enjoy it! But I made up for lost time when I married a transport pilot, a wonderful man named Mark. He taught me things I never knew before and now that I think of all the happiness and thrills I could have had instead of walking that straight line which had been drilled into my head for many years—that's why I say homosexuals, lesbians, French people, or anybody that enjoys sex—

live it up as you're only here for a short time. Do whatever you or your body enjoys. Whether it's in your home or outside because it's nobody's business as you only walk once through this patch of road.

In the end, I was only married for a year. But because of Mark, no one ever looked good to me again. I'm still in love with that one guy. He was tall, 6 foot 1, black curly hair and big green eyes and when he held you, there was no world, there was just the two of us. Mark was a pilot in the Transport Command. These pilots would carry anything that was needed by the Armed Forces. We had a party at our home the night he took off for his last trip. I'll never forget it, we had so much fun. I noticed him talking to Margaret Lindsay, if you remember her, and I said, "What are you two talking about?" Mark, that husband of mine, had a premonition he wasn't coming back. He told this to Margaret. He said, "I better get to this gal of mine before the Western Union telegraph or government sends her a telegram which reads, 'We regret to inform you...'" That's how all messages start out when you lose somebody dear to you.

I'm afraid to tell the rest because you may think the men with the white coats are catching up to me. A few nights later, about three o'clock in the morning, I sat up in my bed and screamed so loud I think they could have heard me a mile away. My eyes were wide open and I was staring at an envelope dangling in front of me in mid-air. I knew instantly that Mark was gone. My next-door neighbor heard the scream and came running in. "Dottie, Dottie, what's wrong with you?"

I said, "Mark was just killed." She said, "How do you know this? Were you notified?" I said, "Yes, I was notified by Mark himself."

I have spoken to people who know about this sort of thing. They said this very rarely happens. They said the channel between me and Mark was wide open. That's how he got to me first.

Dottie Ponedel walking to work on the Paramount lot in the late 1930s.

There were a couple of his uniforms which were supposed to be sent out to be cleaned. I never sent them out because there was a certain smell in them that made me think Mark was still around.

But I got over it the same as other people did, losing their loved ones in that goddamned war.

I remember when Dietrich had my horoscope written out by the same man that did hers. He said that I was very psychic and there was just a hair between me being a genius—I never laughed so hard in my life as when I heard that remark.

But, you know, I've had more of these crazy things happen to me. Sometimes I hear my mother calling me outside of my window. When she starts off, it's a very sweet, low voice and if I don't awaken, she goes off with a hard, loud voice and calls me "Dorothy," my birth name, but she's the only one that ever calls me Dorothy so I know it's her.

Do you know who else is a little psychic? My good pal Joan Blondell. She knew Mark very well. She often said to me, "Where did you find that guy?" After Mark had been dead for some time, Joan called me about 2:30 in the morning and said, "Dottie, get in touch with that husband of yours and tell him to stop pulling my arm. He's trying to get me out of this bed. He doesn't want me sleeping with Todd. I know he never liked Mike but he is scaring the pants off of me. Explain to him that Mike and I are married now and to lay off of me."

3.

My Wonderful Judy

Now that Judy Garland has taken her final trip over the rainbow, it's up to me to write the story that Judy and I were going to write together. I was with Judy a quarter of a century and if she wasn't at my house or me at hers, or on the phone, I always knew what she was up to.

Few people meant more to me in my life than Judy Garland. All of these people who have written about Judy ought to drop dead, because there is no truth to anything they've said. They are just trying to make a dollar on her even though she's gone. But to me, Judy is not dead, she will always live and these people who write about her, even her husbands, never knew Judy like I did. They write that Louis B. Mayer watched her food, which is a lie, because I'm the one who ordered her food and we had big lunches. Steaks, egg salad, anything Judy wanted, we had. And as far as taking marijuana, dope, the needle, or anything that these people wrote about, it's a goddamn lie as the only thing Judy would take was Benzedrine if she had a hard day. She would also take a sleeping pill, but who hasn't? The only needle I ever saw go into Judy's arm was glucose from the doctor because the studio insisted that she be there but Judy was pretty tired and didn't want to eat. The glucose seemed to pep her up.

I wish Judy were here to put a libel suit on these S.O.B.'s. Those who were close to Judy knew that she was one of the greatest comediennes of all time. She would stretch her mouth with both thumbs and cross her eyes and say, "Mirror, mirror, on the wall, am I not the most beautiful of them all?"

But wait, I forgot to tell you how I met Judy.

After being under contract with Paramount for 10 years, I started to lose all my stars as they drifted off to different studios. Jack Dawn, head of the make-up department at MGM heard that my contract was up and asked if I would like to work under him. I said I would and my first assignment was Lucille Ball. Lucille said, "Now come on, Dottie, make me look beautiful."

She seemed nervous that morning. I said, "Lucille, what's up? I can feel you're ready to jump out of this chair."

She said, "As soon as this picture is over, I'm going to Reno to divorce the Cuban." They must have had a hot fight the night before but by the next morning, Lucy told me how much she loved Desi and that everything was rosy again.

Just then, Sydney Guillaroff, head hairdresser, knocked on the door and said, "Can I come in?" I was just finishing working on Lucy and I noticed somebody behind Sydney. He turned toward this person and said, "Now, Judy, this is Dottie who is noted for her glamour make-up. Don't open your mouth until she finishes you. Then you can say whatever you like."

That was the first time I met Judy. Judy opened her hand toward me and in her hands were little rubber discs and tooth caps. I said, "What are these for?"

She said, "The little rubber discs go in my nose and the caps go over my teeth."

I told her, "I don't see anything wrong with your nose and your teeth look perfect to me. Let's put these things in the drawer and forget about them."

I remember one of my first adventures with Judy. She was working on a picture with Fanny Brice that would be released a bit later called *Ziegfeld Follies* (1945). Judy knew Brice from when they worked together in a film called *Everybody Sing* (1938) when she was a kid. We were shooting the Ziegfeld picture during the war right when it was announced that meat was going to be rationed.

One day, an assistant called for Fanny to appear before the camera, but there was no Fanny. People went to look for her all over the studio but nobody could find her. Judy had a hunch what Fanny might be up to. "Come on, Dottie," Judy said. "Hop in my car and let's take a ride." Earlier that day, Judy had heard Brice worrying about how she was going to feed her two children once the meat rationing took effect. Knowing Fanny, she suspected that she had taken immediate action. We drove to Fanny's home in Beverly Hills and were escorted into the kitchen.

When we saw what was happening in that fancy house, Judy and I both became hysterical. Fanny had gone down to the Central Meat Market and had purchased the equivalent of two whole cows. She brought a butcher from the market back home with her and he was cutting up the meat right there in her kitchen, blood flying everywhere, and then wrapping pieces to fill her freezer—it was actually enough to fill several freezers! Fanny was going to see that her kids were going to have meat come hell or high water. Even the butcher who was cutting up the meat said to us, "This could only happen once in a lifetime!"

I knew that Judy was worming herself right into my heart when she said to me, "You know, Dottie, I've been looking for something like you for a long time." I knew what she meant. She was looking for that love she never got.

Dottie and Judy began their friendship in the make-up room
but they became lifelong confidantes.

Don't forget Judy was on the stage at three. Judy and I became like mother and daughter. She once said to me, "How does it feel to be indispensable?" I said, "There is no such thing as being indispensable. There is always somebody to take your place."

But not in the case of Judy Garland. There was nobody to follow this girl. When God dished out talent, she got way more than her share. Judy could take an audience and twist it and turn it, stand them up on their ear and the crowds would holler for more.

I used to love going with Judy to the recording studio at MGM to listen to her pre-record her songs for a picture. After finishing a song, Judy would come over to me. She could always tell by the look in my eye whether she hit the top or not. It got to the point where Johnny Green, the orchestra conductor, would look over at me as if to say, "Is that okay?" or, "Can she do better?" But often when she sang her heart out on those numbers, the whole orchestra would be up on its feet applauding her over and over. Sometimes I'd see our producer, Arthur Freed, in the corner with tears falling right down on his cheeks. Oh boy, Judy moved everyone in that recording room.

I remember one night when I walked into the Minnelli house, there was Arthur Freed talking to Minnelli about a picture called *The Clock* (1945). He said, "I've got a present for you, Judy," as he placed the script into her hands.

Minnelli was to direct Judy and Robert Walker would be her leading man. Judy was thrilled to get a real dramatic role with no singing, but it was a hard picture to do. Walker was in a strange frame of mind as he had recently lost his wife Jennifer Jones to David O. Selznick. He was drinking pretty heavily and we never knew if he was going to show up the next morning or not.

Judy's heart was with Walker. One day, when he was nowhere to be found, Judy asked me to help her hunt him down. We eventually did find him and I could immediately tell that he had hit the bottle pretty bad. He didn't seem to care at all that we were in the middle of doing a picture, he was just out. Judy was the best Florence Nightingale that ever drew breath. She stayed with Walker, got him on his feet, and the next morning he was on the set with no trouble at all.

Walker was the happiest guy when his two little boys would visit him on the set. They were the most beautiful two boys you have ever seen. He was so proud of them. Everything seemed to go so smoothly on the picture for a while—we were all helping Walker get through it. Sometimes Walker and Judy would come to my house after a long day at the studio.

"Gee, Dottie," he told me one night when we got some food and black coffee into him after another binge. "It's a privilege to come to your house where it's so peaceful. Is there anything you need? Let me go out and buy it for you."

"I don't need anything," I told him. "I just want you to stay sober until the end of this picture."

Talking about Robert Walker reminds me of the time a few years later when I was driving home with Vincente and Judy. Vincente said, "By the way, Dottie, I put in a call to have you do a test for me on Jennifer Jones."

I said, "Vincente, even if I could make Jennifer look like Venus de Milo, I still wouldn't be able to do your picture."

"Why not?" Judy asked.

"Because I heard through the grapevine that there are two guys who have a knife in my back a foot deep and they are friends of Selznick's—one of them is a make-up man and one a hairdresser. They told Selznick that I would make Jennifer look like Dietrich and take away all her girlish charm. They also told him I was a lesbian which is the goddamnedest lie ever."

"You're going to do the test tomorrow," Vincente said. I did the test and when Minnelli saw it, he said he thought Jennifer Jones looked like a Dresden doll, she was so beautiful. But I didn't end up doing the picture because a letter came from Selznick saying he wanted his own hairdresser and make-up man to do it, just as I suspected would happen. But he had to admit that was one of the prettiest tests he had ever seen of her.

I can't even count all the crazy adventures I had with Judy over the years. My night in Chinatown with Judy was something to remember. She came to me and said, "There's a place in Chinatown that makes shrimp as big as your head. We're going there tonight. It is run by a family with four boys and two girls and a mother and father who do the cooking. This Chinese restaurant is the talk of the town. I'm going to dress like a bum and put on a blonde wig so nobody will recognize me. Now, Dottie, don't put any make-up on and kind of look lousy so nobody will pay any attention to us."

When Judy got through with herself, she looked like she was ready to go trick-or-treating. We got in the car and headed for Chinatown. We found the place and got ourselves seated. When we were asked what we'd like to order, we said, "Bring us everything that's good and don't forget the shrimp." Well, we had seven different types of food and a double order of shrimp. We sat there and ate and ate and ate. When the boy started to pick up the empty dishes, the button on his sleeve caught on Judy's wig and pulled it down into her face. Judy calmly parted the hair in front of her face and looked up at the boy. His eyes opened wide as he recognized her but Judy put her finger up to her lips and shook her head. When he went back into the kitchen, we could tell that he had told the family that Judy Garland was out there because one by one we could see their heads poking out of the doorway.

By this time, the whole thing struck Judy as funny and she got a laughing jag on. The boy came back out and Judy told him to bring out an entire order of what we had just eaten and to put it in small cartons so we could take it home. He also brought out an extra large bag of fortune cookies and gave it to her on the house. He said, "This is from me to you." He was so cute that I thought Judy was going to take him home with her.

We put the stuff in our car and I think there was enough food to last us for a week. When we got home to my house, Judy threw herself on the bed and I threw myself on the couch in the den and we both dozed off because we were so full of food. We slept until I heard a noise in the kitchen about 3:30 am. When I got out there, Judy had every carton opened and there was a big spoon in each one. There was a big highball sitting alongside her. Judy said, "Oh, Dottie, I knew this stuff was out here and I just had to get to it."

I said, "Okay, just clean up this mess before you go to bed."

When I got up a few hours later and checked the kitchen, there was food everywhere. When I peeked in the bedroom, there was Queen Judy snoring her head off. Now I had to get into that kitchen and clean up the mess!

That afternoon, we took it easy because we didn't have to report to the studio for a couple of days. We were sunbathing in the patio when in walked Ava Gardner and Howard Duff with corned beef sandwiches and Cokes and a big bunch of pickles. A little later, Arthur Freed stopped by. Seeing our little party in the patio, he joined right in. Those were fun years, all right.

Judy reminded me of someone who gets shot out of a cannon and then flies through the air and never stops. We did one picture after another together: *Meet Me in St. Louis* (1944), *The Clock* (1945), *Ziegfeld Follies* (1945), *The Harvey Girls* (1946), and it went on from there. In those days, it was an honor to work under the MGM banner. It was considered one of the top studios. Some of the stars would cut their salaries just to be under contract to MGM.

The studio worked Judy like a horse. If Arthur Freed wasn't ready with a new picture for Judy, Joe Pasternak was. These were two of the biggest producers of musicals at MGM and they kept Judy riding on a treadmill. If she wasn't shooting, she was rehearsing or learning new songs or dances, they had her going all the time. It's a wonder she didn't jump out of her skin but being Judy, with a constitution made of steel, she was equal to the task. I don't think anybody could turn out as many pictures as Judy did for MGM. She made millions for them and wound up penniless. But that was mostly because she had no head for business.

Judy never knew the value of a dollar. That's why everybody took advantage of her. She never knew where her money was going. I tried to sit her down with pencil and paper and show her figures of what she should have been able to save that year but Judy looked up at me and said, "Dottie, I'll always be able to make a dollar so what's the use of worrying?"

"Dottie—Stay with me, baby. I love you. Judy"

I said, "Judy, you know if I could get part of Mae West's brain and part of Paulette Goddard's brain and put them into your brain, you could be President of the United States. Because Miss West and

Miss Goddard could turn this land of ours into a Shangri-La if they had a mind to. Judy, if you were as smart as Paulette you'd have a couple million under your belt by now."

"So what if I did?" Judy said. "Somebody would always be there to take it away from me."

"Yeah, Judy," I replied. "The man upstairs gave you a world of talent but not a bit of smarts for business."

"Oh, Dottie, I know I'm going to wind up behind the eight ball but look how much fun I'm having while I'm doing it! You know," she told me, "I'd be smart if I made you my business manager. Except you'd put every dime I made into government bonds, I wouldn't even have enough money to eat on."

"You think that would be bad, Judy?"

"No, not bad," Judy said, "but then I wouldn't be me because brains and talent never go together and I'd much rather have talent."

"Oh don't worry, Judy, you were in line twice while they were dishing that out. The Man upstairs was sure good to you as you sure know how to belt it out and always keep that little cry in your voice as you sing because your public loves it."

Judy had a beautiful dressing room at the studio, including a big square bed covered in blue satin. One day, I was sitting on the bed and Judy came over and put her head on my shoulder. "Dottie, you know I'm not pretending," she said. "They think I'm making it up but I'm so tired." I could tell she'd never make it through that day but the studio wasn't buying it.

I said, "Judy, start coughing and drink some real hot water while I call the studio nurse." When the nurse knocked on the dressing room door, Judy drank the water, almost scalding. When the nurse stuck the thermometer in Judy's mouth, her temperature was 102.

The nurse said, "Judy, you must be coming down with the flu." She called the producer and said, "If you don't send Judy home now, you won't have her for a week." As long as the studio nurse verified it, the studio believed it. That gave Judy a couple of days to play with her baby daughter, Liza. I would love to have pulled that scheme for her every few weeks but that would have been too dangerous.

Dottie was a regular fixture at the Minnellis' home and spent a lot of time with Liza who was born in 1946. Baby Liza loved the faces Dottie would make for her benefit—she may have been making them while this photo was taken.

After a couple of days, Judy was on the set, working her butt off, and in walked Louis B. Mayer. He walked over, put his arms around me, and I could feel the whole set starting to buzz. Some of them probably thought I was playing hanky-panky with the boss but that wasn't the case. He just wanted to thank me for watching out for Judy and getting her to the set on time. He knew that I loved Judy and that I would always watch out for her. I would fight the studio producers and anybody else that would go against Judy, I was like a bear with its cub.

Mr. Mayer said, "I've heard a lot about you, Dottie."

"I hope it's good," I said, remembering the little trick I had pulled a few days before.

"Stop at the cashier's office before you leave today," Mr. Mayer said. "There's a surprise for you there."

"Ooh, run over there quick!" Judy said, "I want to find out what it is. I hope it's a million dollars!"

Mr. Mayer laughed and said, "It's just a little something to keep her happy."

I think I made that cashier's window in one big step since I was just as anxious as Judy to see what I got. Paul, the cashier, said, "Dottie how do you rate a bonus check like this?" It was $500! Mr. Mayer was still on the set when I got back. I walked over to him and kissed him on the cheek and showed Judy the check.

Judy said to him, "You could have doubled that and the studio would never miss it."

He said, "Well, she will get a surprise after every picture you do," and he lived up to that. The thing that Judy and I didn't know was that Judy's mother, Ethel, was in Mr. Mayer's office earlier that day asking him to fire me. She said that I was a bad influence on Judy which, of course, was a lie as big as they come. Ethel was jealous of the love Judy had for me.

Dottie and Judy on the set of *The Harvey Girls* (1946) just before shooting the
scene featuring that year's Academy Award winner for Best Song, "On the
Atchison, Topeka, and the Santa Fe."

Judy would call me "mom" every once in a while, especially when
she wasn't feeling well. From the moment we met, I gave Judy the love
her mother should have given her. I often said to Judy, "Your mother
loves you in her own peculiar way. Why don't you bend a little bit?"

Judy said, "Some day I'll tell you why I can't bend."

One day, Jerry Mayer, Louis B. Mayer's brother and the head of production, sent for me. As I walked in his office, I was dumbstruck because I never saw such a beautiful place. I kept turning until I got to his desk, like I was doing some kind of dance. I started worrying why I was called in to his office.

"Am I fired?" I asked.

He handed me an envelope and said, "Dottie, you have done a good job. Stick with it!"

I said, "If this is a check, I can't take it, because your brother gave me a bonus check two weeks ago, and whatever you're going to give me, it isn't worth losing my job."

Jerry sat back in his chair and laughed. "Dottie, don't you know I know every check that goes out of here? Now be a good girl, take it, and have fun."

I tore open the envelope when I got out of there and it was the same amount that Mr. Mayer had given me two weeks earlier: $500!

During this time, I remember trying to solve the mystery of who was regularly leaving a long-stemmed American Beauty rose in Judy's dressing room. Each morning, we arrived at work to find a single rose on Judy's desk. It must have been put there really early in the morning, even before the prop men arrived. This had been going on for about two months and we still didn't know who was doing it. Every time we opened the dressing room door, there it was, staring us in the face. Judy suggested we sleep in the dressing room that night. I said, "What will Vincente think?" Judy said that he'd think we were nuts and let it go at that.

Well, we stayed in her dressing room that night and at about 6:00 the next morning, the cop from the front gate came strolling in with the rose! He didn't see us as he came in. As we watched him put the rose in a vase, Judy suddenly piped up. "So you're the one who's putting the rose here every morning!" The cop denied it.

"Not me! The florist brings it to me and I put it in your room. Orders from Joe Pasternak."

I told Judy, "When Joe comes to the set, give him a big kiss and tell him you know all about the rose and if he asks you how you know, just say you slept here all night to see who was doing it." Judy did just that and thanked him. Pasternak said that there'd be a rose coming every day until we finished that picture.

Judy Garland (in the front row) with the crew from
The Harvey Girls (1946) including Dottie (fifth from left in
the second row). Dottie worked with Judy on 10 films at MGM.

To work with Judy was a joy and a privilege, and it was one surprise after another. Sometimes I would hold Judy so tight she couldn't even breathe and when she used to raise those goose-pimples in me with her performances, I could just cry.

Shooting so many films in a row was grueling work, but
Dottie and Judy always found time for a laugh.

Judy was never afraid to tell me anything whether it was a happy or sad thought. She never pulled any punches with me, she would always tell me whatever went on in that bed of hers with whatever husband she had at the time. Sometimes I would go into a laughing fit with the funny tales she would tell me but that was Judy; whatever she wanted to tell me she would blabber it out and she was never ashamed to tell me the way she felt about it. If her husbands only knew the secrets that Judy had told me they would have dodged me every time they saw me. There were no secrets between Judy and me. I was like a big old hen with my wings spread out with Judy under them for protection.

Sometimes Judy would have hard nights—walking around her house by herself, one room to the other. If things got too tough, she'd get me on the phone at two or three in the morning. Sometimes she felt so alone that she said she had to come over to see me. Judy had a way of slipping out of bed, getting in her car, and coming over no matter what time it was and no matter what husband it was—who was going to argue with Judy? It was like arguing with City Hall, you just can't win.

It didn't take long until the front doorbell rang and I'd holler, "Okay, Judy, waltz yourself in, the door is open!" Under her arm would be a bottle of scotch and a bag of corned beef sandwiches. Judy always stopped off at an all-night delicatessen and filled up a bag of goodies and I knew then and there that there would be no sleep that night.

Judy decided she needed to get away from her marriage to Vincente Minnelli for a while and rent a nice little house for herself so she could do as she wanted for a couple of months.

"Why don't you talk it over with Vincente?" I asked.

"I know it will be fine with him," she said. "I've been impossible to live with lately."

Judy put her secretary to work to find a house for her but she didn't like anything we saw. Finally, Katie Hepburn told Judy about a house she saw for rent to the tune of $1100 a month. We went up to see it and Judy said, "This is for me." The following week, we were in that hideaway of hers. The warmth of a large fireplace, candlelight, the smell of wildflowers dripping out of a vase, good food on the table, as many highballs as you could want—who's going to complain about an atmosphere like that? If you closed your eyes you could picture yourself in any part of the world you wanted to be.

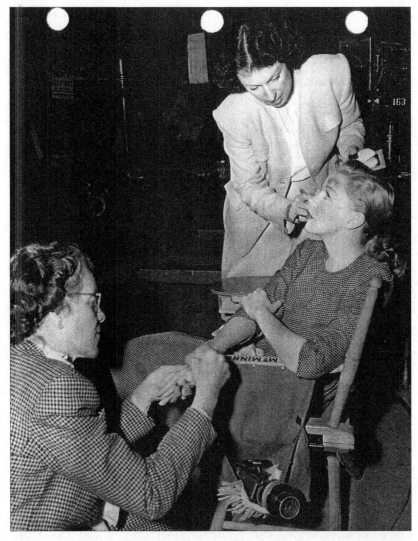

Dottie applying the finishing touches on Judy for her scene singing "Look for the Silver Lining" as Ziegfeld star Marilyn Miller in *Till the Clouds Roll By* (1946).

Except the only place where Judy wanted to be was in Frank Sinatra's arms. Way back in that brain of hers she was planning this the whole time. Judy had a secret yen for Frank. She loved to hear him sing, tell jokes, and cut up the way he used to. Judy said, "Let's make a nice dinner tomorrow with all the trimmings. Dottie, you call Frank, you know how to do it."

I knew Frank admired her as an artist. He always said she was the tops in show business but when it came to making love to Judy, he didn't want to get involved. I tried so hard and called every place I thought he would be, just to come up and have dinner and spend an evening with her. But no matter where I called, they said he wasn't there and I knew damn well he was. Deep in Frank's heart, he was scared to death of Judy.

Judy asked me once, "Why do some fellas run the other way when they see me coming?"

"The reason is, Judy, that you become so overpowering that they can't fight you back."

One night in that little house, Judy seemed very relaxed. She turned to me and said, "Dottie, please don't ever leave me." She started dancing around the room and said, "I'm going to do some imitations for you." She knew I was her best audience.

Judy ran into the kitchen, got a big white bowl, and put it on her head to take the place of a big straw hat. She threw out her lower lip and started to sing "Louise" in a broken French accent. I wish everyone could have seen this—it would have given the world the laugh it needed as Judy clowned this Chevalier bit to the hilt.

Judy went back home with Minnelli soon after that night, but I could see that she was restless. She often fell in love with her leading men and always wanted to know what made them tick. As we were walking toward her dressing room after work one day, she said, "Dottie, you know what's wrong with me? I need a new romance." I said, "Judy, don't start that again." Judy said, "I'm tired of the same routine. The studio, then home, then the studio, then home, day after day."

I knew the fireworks were going to start that night. But Judy and Vincente went to a party at Ira Gershwin's home. Ira Gershwin was the brother of George Gershwin who was a dear friend of Vincente's. Judy seemed to enjoy that party as the next day she was her old self again and said, "Dottie, I'm going up to talk to Mr. Mayer to see if we can get some time off to go to New York and see the shows there."

When she came down, she had a red nose and red eyes. Mr. Mayer had told her that a vacation would have to wait until later in the year—but Judy wanted it now. She said, "Dottie, would you like to bet me we'll be in New York in a couple of weeks?"

"I wouldn't bet you anything, Judy, because you can bore through a steel wall when you want something."

That night, I went straight home from the studio. At about 1:30 in the morning, the phone rang and Judy was on the other end, sounding strange. She said, "Don't worry, Dottie, it's not as bad as it seems." Judy had cut both her wrists but not deep enough to hurt her, just enough for blood to come to the surface. Judy never wanted to die, she just wanted to scare the pants off everybody to have her own way. Judy never did anything like that unless there was somebody around to feel sorry for her and love her. Judy was always searching for something she wanted but she didn't really know what it was.

By the time I got to the Minnellis' house, the doctor had arrived and her wrists were bandaged. It seemed like half the studio bosses were there. Judy only had about a week to finish the picture and they were all worried. I said, "I'll cover up those two little bandages with make-up. I'm sure we'll be on the set in the morning."

To everyone's surprise, we were ready for a full day's work the next day but Judy said, "We're going to leave Hollywood for good and take off for New York."

I said, "Judy, don't talk that way about Hollywood. It was very good to you and to me."

As we sat in her dressing room having our lunch, Judy said, "Dottie, why have I got such a lousy reputation with the extra people? Whenever they get a call for my picture, I hear they always ask the casting office if there is anything else besides Judy's picture, yet my pictures give them more work than any other pictures on this lot."

"Well, Judy," I said, "take today, for instance. Nobody thought you were going to show up for work after what happened last night. If you hadn't shown up with a couple of hundred people on call, they would have been cancelled and these people would have told a couple hundred other people and that's how your reputation begins to stink. But don't let that get you down, Judy. You're still number one at the box office."

"You know, Dottie, I'm not afraid to ask you anything. You always give me a sensible, direct answer. You never try to butter up anything for me. That's why I feel you're a part of me. I always considered myself an ugly duckling until I saw the close-up of myself in the window scene of *Meet Me In St Louis*. As you always say to me, "feel beautiful and you will be beautiful." I promise I'll be a good girl and not give you any more trouble. Just love me like you do Dietrich."

I replied, "Do you know, Judy, I couldn't love you any more if I had born you into this world. I seem to be an old hen with my wings stretched out where you're concerned."

One Christmas at the Minnelli house when we were all sitting around the Christmas tree, Judy handed me a big box. It was filled with paper and when I got down to the bottom of it, I found a little mesh purse. I looked at both of them questioningly and Judy said, "Alright, schnook, open it up." I turned the little knob on the purse and inside was a $500 bill. Was my face red! I had thought they were playing a practical joke on me. I never saw so many presents under the tree as I did that morning and poor Pearl, the Minnellis' house-keeper, had a heck of a time cleaning it all up. The Christmas tree was all lit up and the top of it hit the ceiling. The fireplace was aglow as we sat in front of it eating a wonderful Christmas breakfast. We made Pearl sit down with us.

Wouldn't it be wonderful if every day could be Christmas? It seems everyone has more compassion and love and maybe they're a little afraid of the Man upstairs on this day.

Sitting there with these two people, I suddenly realized I was sitting with two giants. Judy, a giant in her profession, and Vincente, a top director, a giant in his own right. We were sitting back on the sofa with our feet on the coffee table as though we didn't have a care in the world.

I loved all of my time with Judy, even the difficult times. To know Judy was to love her. Whenever that phone would ring, I would see Judy's face in the mouthpiece; she really had me humming even when she wasn't with me. Oh boy, how I loved that girl, come hell or high water. I loved her when she laughed and I loved her when she cried. I loved the trouble she got into, I loved all the pranks she pulled, I loved watching those wheels go around in her head because I knew I would have to follow-up to get her out of all these messes and believe me, that was okay by me.

Dottie with flamboyant actress Peggy Hopkins Joyce on the set
of *International House* (1933). In addition to working closely with
Marlene Dietrich, many of the female stars at Paramount fought
for her services during the 1930s.

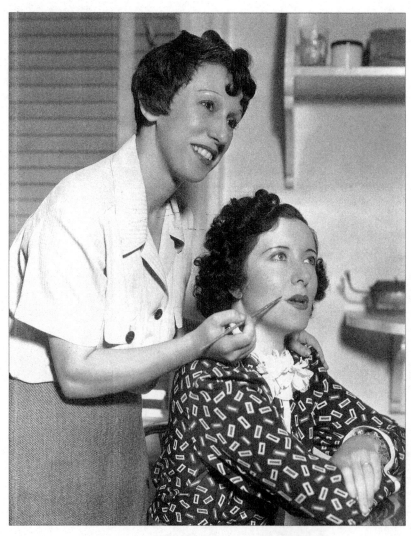

Ponedel also worked with Gracie Allen during the
making of *International House* (1933).

Dottie helped transform her friend Adrienne Ames into a true
glamour queen at Paramount. Like Dottie, Ames had started as a
stand-in during the silent movie era. "For that wild Indian
Ponedel—I couldn't get along without her! Adrienne"

Another portrait of Adrienne Ames that clearly shows the magic of Ponedel's make-up artistry. "For Dot—Howza 'bout it." Affectionately, Adrienne"

Dottie worked with Lillian Roth in the early 1930s, whose life was later told in the film *I'll Cry Tomorrow* (1955) starring Susan Hayward. "To darling Dot, The girl I owe a lot to. You've been a peach. I'll never forget your sweetness. Always most sincerely, Lillian Roth"

Lilyan Tashman was a star in vaudeville, on Broadway, and in the movies.
Dottie worked with her shortly before her untimely death in 1934.
"For Dot—In appreciation of a really great artist with all
my thanks and love. Lilyan Tashman"

Metropolitan Opera diva Gladys Swarthout was Paramount's answer to Jeanette MacDonald after MacDonald left the studio for MGM. Dot worked with Swarthout on several of her pictures and remained in touch with the singer for many years. "To Dot, of the swift, sure, gentle fingers, with appreciation."

Many of the industry's biggest stars were thrilled to find themselves in Dottie's expert hands. "To Dot—To remind you of a number of good times. Love, Margaret Sullavan"

Many of the stars Dottie worked with remain household names
today, while others, such as Judith Barrett, are largely forgotten.
"To my good friend Dot, with many thanks for your interest
and artistry. (Is my mouth on straight?) Judith"

Dottie's younger brother, Bernard "Beans" Ponedel, followed her to Paramount and then to MGM. He later became Frank Sinatra's primary make-up artist.

Joan Blondell remained one of Dottie's closest friends for life. Dottie knew Joan
through all three of her marriages. Here she is with husband Dick Powell.

Dottie spent a lot of time with Joan's young children, Ellen and Norman Powell. Joan signed this photograph, "For Dotty, I made 'em!! —Joan"

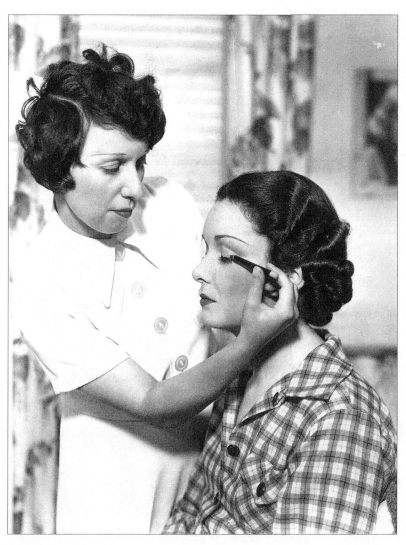

Actress Gail Patrick was another friend for life, continuing to visit Dottie regularly long after leaving the movie business.

Gail Patrick made her last film in 1948, but later became a successful television producer of shows such as *Perry Mason*. "To my little Dottie, from a friend who will always be indebted to you. Lovingly, Gail"

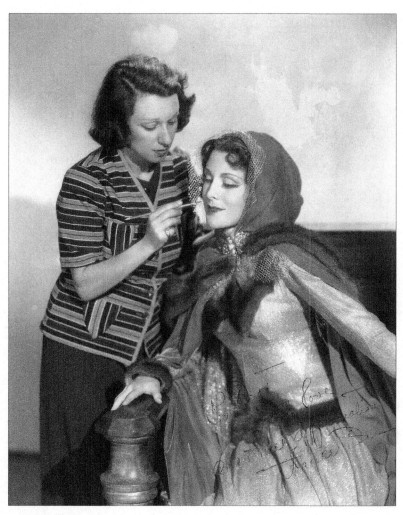

Frances Dee also became one of Dottie's good friends, along with Dee's
husband, Joel McCrea. Frances often visited Dottie's Beverly Hills home.
"To Dot, with love and much appreciation."

Martha Raye helping Dottie celebrate her birthday on the Paramount lot.
Dottie was actually born on July 2, but she liked to say that she was born on the
Fourth of July—thus the little American flags on her birthday cake!

Though she had problems with the territorial male heads of the make-up department, Dottie was loved by the cast and crew of all the films she worked on.

By the late 1930s, articles started appearing about Dot Ponedel's
immense talents. Here she is in her Paramount make-up room
being interviewed by an Australian journalist.

"Follow the natural line of the brow when applying your make-up,
and use a fine camel's hair brush for removing traces of powder.
Dot Ponedel, Paramount studio make-up expert, gives Dolores Casey,
Paramount player in *Café Society* (1939), a few pointers on the correct
method of applying make-up. The finishing touch is supplied by
'patting' on a thin coat of face powder with a soft powder puff."

Many of Dottie's friends, including Paulette Goddard, spent a lot of time in Dot's Paramount office in the 1930s. Notice the photos of Marlene Dietrich and Judith Barrett in the background.

One of the many photographs Judy Garland inscribed to her dear friend.
"To Dot, My dreamy character. With all my love—Judy"

When Ginger Rogers reteamed with Fred Astaire for MGM's *The Barkleys of Broadway* (1949), she insisted that Dottie do her make-up. The head of MGM's make-up department fought it, but Ginger persevered and Dottie got the job.

4.

Judy and I Hightail It Out of Town

In 1948, MGM wanted to send Judy on a cross-country train trip to publicize her upcoming picture, *The Pirate*. Myrtle Tully, Judy's secretary, and I were to go with her. Tully was steady and reliable and would handle all the day-to-day dealings such as ordering tickets, arranging Judy's trunks, and, in general, making sure everything was taken care of. I was to make sure Judy stayed on an even keel.

Judy was excited about the trip—really looking forward to getting away for a while as her recent shooting schedule had exhausted her. She was hoping to let loose on this trip and didn't want anything or anyone to get in her way, including me. She made it clear to me that I could stay close—but not too close. I knew I was going to have my hands full. At one point, I reminded her that Liza had been a Caesarian birth and there were only so many one woman was allowed to have.

"Don't you know, Dottie, women can have up to three C-sections now."

I wasn't buying it. "Judy, I don't give a damn if they raise it to 50! I don't want to be around when it happens."

"But you will be," she said. "I definitely want more kids. There's no way I'm going to stop at one but I don't think they're going to be with Vincente because I'm ready to fly that coop now. Tomorrow is the last day of the picture and we're not scheduled to do another one for a long time and that should make you happy. Hello, New York, here we come!"

Dottie and Judy on the set of *The Pirate* (1948)
just before taking off for their New York adventure.

Tully had ordered a suite of rooms at the Carlton Hotel. Oh boy, we were really going to live in high cotton. I knew the studio would have a big black limousine at our disposal with a chauffeur, and I knew they'd have a man assigned to us to keep us out of trouble. They did that for every star while under contract so there'd be somebody to meet us in Chicago and somebody in New York.

There was this one place I wanted to make sure to eat at in New York and that was Le Pavillion because only the rich could afford to eat there and once you threw your hat in, you had a beautiful bill staring you in the face but we were going to try it because everything goes on this trip.

As we got into the car at the studio, Judy said, "Let's stop at Don Loper's and see if he's got something pretty I can wear. Or should I wait until we get to New York to go on a buying spree?"

I told her, "Judy, we only have three more days to go on this picture and then we'll be off for New York. I'm sure if the studio knows where we're at, they won't worry too much in case of retakes. We can always fly back in a couple of hours."

Judy said, "Do you think we're counting our chickens before they hatch?"

I said, "No, Judy, I think you won this round because I think the bosses know you want to finish this picture on time."

Judy said, "Whether the studio says yes or no, Tully, you, and I are going to be on that train headed for New York. Tell Tully to get out of slow motion, get our tickets, pack my clothes, and, if necessary, I'll put a firecracker under her to get her going. Dottie, I have a hunch we're going to have one hell of a time in New York. Maybe it will get some of this craziness out of my system. And maybe I can find a part-time romance."

I could tell the wheels were starting to turn in that head of Judy's. I was wondering to myself, can I keep up with this kid? What I should really do is go to sleep for 20 years.

"Alright, Judy, why don't you count your blessings? Go home and have some fun with Liza. She's probably waiting for you."

"Dottie, you know damn well she's waiting to see if you're coming over because you're the one she's always looking for," Judy said, laughing. "Come on and have some dinner with Vincente and me, play with Liza for an hour, and then you can go home."

I said, "If I do go home, I don't want you calling me at two in the morning telling me you can't sleep, because I'm going to take the receiver off the hook."

"Dottie, don't do that because I'll have Western Union at your front door to tell you to put it back on again."

"I got all my things packed and I know Tully's been packing your things for the last three days. She has our tickets for that old Santa Fe."

"Whoopee!" Judy said. "I am going to let loose and nobody better stop me or get in my way. Now I have to get some Benzedrine, Miltown, and sleeping pills."

"Judy," I said. "If you take any of those things with you, I'm not going. I'll be way too far from home to throw you in a wooden box."

"Oh Dottie, you know I'm kidding. I don't need anything anymore. You saw to that. With Tully and you on my back, I don't even think I could use a deodorant."

"I remember, Judy, when you came running to me, you were so full of bubble. You couldn't wait to tell me that Vincente asked you to marry him. Your eyes seemed to open up like a full moon. Now you're getting cuckoo looking for other green pastures. Forget this drive you have in you. There must be some kind of monkey on your back steering you the wrong way because the grass always looks greener to you in the next person's yard. Some day you'll realize you have the rainbow right in your hand. Still, knowing you as I do, I'm sure there will be other men, because there is no satisfying you."

"Okay, Dottie," she said. "When I get as old as you, I'll sit myself in a rocking chair and put a corncob pipe in my mouth, sip on some vegetable soup, and call it a day."

"Judy, you can make fun of me if you like, but I hope some day somebody will get to that brain of yours and then you won't have to work when you hit 90," I told her. Just then, the phone rang and it was Tully on the other end, telling me that she found two slack suits for Judy and they were really beautiful.

Later on, at Judy and Vincente's, I said, "I wonder if Mr. Mayer is going to give me that bonus he promised at the end of each picture."

"I'm sure he will," Judy said. "He hasn't failed so far and besides, I'm taking enough money for all of us, so let's end this night playing downstairs in the nursery with Liza."

While Vincente was reading his script, he had his ear cocked toward us to figure out what we were planning. Vincente laughed and said, "I may join you people in New York later on."

Judy said, "Oh no, you're not 'cause this is my vacation and I'm going to put the red carpet out for myself."

After the wrap party at the studio when we were driving home, Judy was feeling happy as a lark and I said, "Judy, just relax and sing my favorite song, "Slow Boat to China." When we got to Judy's, the aroma coming out of Pearl's kitchen was really something. "We better make an effort to eat," I said, "or she is going to feel bad. She went all out knowing this is the last night of the picture. Well, tomorrow night at seven, we'll be on that choo-choo train. Tully got us two staterooms and we'll open the door between them and make one big compartment. I'm going to go home tonight to my little house and get all my chores done, lock up, and get ready for the trip tomorrow."

We spent the next day at the Minnelli house having a lot of fun with Liza. We made a very happy day of it because in a couple of hours we'd be heading for the train. Everything went as smooth as glass. Pearl said, "Can I fix a big bag of goodies for the train?" Judy told her, "Don't you know they have everything from soup to nuts on the train but we'll take it anyway, Pearl." As a couple of hours rolled by, we were kissing Liza and everybody in the house. You would think we were going away forever. Judy gave Vincente a big kiss and said we would be back before they knew it. We jumped in a car and Judy's houseboy rolled us to the station and in about two minutes we were in our double compartments.

The porters bent over backwards when they saw Judy. They were at her beck and call. There wasn't anything on that train that Judy asked for that didn't come knocking on the door. We were served a dinner that was fit for a king and Judy said, "Let's all three of us take our highball glasses and make a wish." She said, "Why is it when we pick up our glasses to anyone, we always say 'Skoal,' 'Happy Days,' or 'Here's to You,' and when a Jewish person picks up his glass, he always says 'L'Chaim?' What does that mean, Dot?"

I told her, "It means 'God bless you, be happy, stay well.' It means everything that is good."

"Alright", Judy said. "Let's order another drink and we'll all say 'L'Chaim!'"

Judy looked over at Tully and said, "Let your hair down and be like Dottie and me and stop being the perfect lady."

Tully said, "Well, if I stop being the perfect lady, who's going to take care of you two? Somebody's got to be in line."

We ate so much and drank and all three of us were on cloud nine, including Tully. Judy said, "Alright, Dottie, now you have to sing me a song."

"Okay," I said. "I'll sing you a Jewish song that my mother taught me when I was a little girl. The name of the song is 'The Tallisel.' Now, the Tallit is a prayer shawl that the men wear in the temple and on their head they wear a yarmulke."

I was just drunk enough to make all those notes come out perfect. I think everybody on that train heard me. Tully and Judy were amazed, they sat there as though a bomb hit them. Judy said, "Dottie, you're in the wrong profession. I'm going to be your manager and you're going to sing."

I replied, "Oh boy, Judy, now I've heard everything." Judy said, "Alright, Tully, now it's your turn."

Tully said, "I don't know how to sing."

"Then recite Humpty Dumpty," Judy said, "but you've got to do something!" Tully had already had a few herself and as she stood up to recite the poem, she landed on the floor.

Judy said, "Okay, get me a ukulele, Dottie, and I'll sing 'Slow Boat to China.'" Judy can sure belt that song out if anybody can and I can listen to her sing that song over and over again.

"Well, we have a couple of days and nights on this train before we hit Chicago," Judy said. "We're going to be loaded but when we get off this train we're going to be perfect ladies so the reporters can't report that we were hitting the champagne bottle. Oh, Dottie, I feel as free as a bird. I want to feel this way all my life. Do you think that can happen to me?"

"Yeah, Judy," I told her. "Anything can happen to you."

As we sat with our faces toward the windows, the trees, the houses, and the telephone poles were passing us like lightning. Judy said, "Look up there, Dottie, quick! See that bird? That's me. I'm as free as the all outdoors and all the gates are far behind me."

"What do you mean, Judy?" I asked.

"I mean the studio. Getting away from it is like taking a cool shower. I feel so good, Dottie, I can't tell you how I feel."

Before we knew it, the train trip was almost over and Tully was screaming her head off, telling us to get some sleep as we were going to hit Chicago in the morning. Judy said, "Okay, Dottie, ring for the porter. I want a deviled egg sandwich and some hot coffee and you can order a chicken salad sandwich and I can take half or yours and you can take half of mine. Tell them to bring potato chips with it."

Tully said, "Well, I've had it with you guys. I might as well sit up and eat, too, there will be no sleep tonight."

Judy laughed and said, "Try to be like us. Stop being so prim and proper and you'll get more laughs out of life."

Soon afterwards, the porter brought in a tray full of goodies. I had seen Judy slip them a big bill when she first got on the train. "Dottie, you only get what you pay for and I want service and I'm going to get it. Now that our bellies are full of food, let's see if we can get a little shut-eye."

It took about 20 minutes and I heard Tully snoring and saw that Judy's eyelids were getting heavy. I figured we'd at least get a few hours of sleep since everything was packed and ready to lift off the train—Tully saw to that. I knew that Mr. Pupsenik, one of the men who takes care of the stars as they come through Chicago, would be waiting for us with a big black limousine at the station. I knew we'd be heading for the Ambassador East as the penthouse was waiting. When you travel with a star, you get the best of everything, especially with Judy. There would be champagne and flowers in her room when we got there. They generally put out a big spread for Judy so I knew we'd be living in high cotton for at least a week.

The next thing I knew, the porter was banging on our door saying we were in Chicago, everybody needed to get up, and that was just the time when all three of us wanted to sleep! Boy, we got in each other's way trying to hurry, because we didn't know if the press would be out there or not. Judy kept asking, "How do I look, Dot, how do I look?" and I said, "You look like a perfect lady, now act like one and be very friendly, because the press loves that and don't be nasty to any of them. If you say one wrong word, they'll add 10 more to it . So make a big *tzimmis* over all of them and hello them to death and you will be the little Judy that never grew up."

Judy looked out the window and there was Mr. Pupsenik and a big new Cadillac waiting for us. As we stepped off the train, we looked like ready money because Tully was wearing an Irene suit which cost about 300 bucks and I had found some stunning clothes of Judy's which she had never worn. It was my luck being the same size that Judy was. We all acted very friendly and very joyous.

Judy turned around to me and said, "How am I doing, Dot?"

I said, "Just fine. Keep it up." And before we knew it, we were at the hotel and we were ushered up to the penthouse of the Ambassador East. That was about the swankiest place in Chicago. Tully was unpacking our things when I heard a knock at the door.

There was a good-looking guy in the doorway. He said, "Hello, Judy." He happened to be one of the sons of the owner of either Gimbel's or Macy's in New York, I can't remember which but boy, was he loaded! He said, "Judy, I'm here for a couple of weeks to paint the town red. Do you want to join me?"

Judy looked up at him and said, "Just let me have a nice hot shower and I'll meet you down in the Pump Room in an hour." Judy got dolled up and looked like a million bucks. She walked into the Pump Room and nobody noticed her. Her date walked up to her and escorted her to a table in the corner of the room where the lights were dim, hoping that the autograph hounds would leave her alone but lo and behold, one of the boys in the band noticed her and started to play "Over the Rainbow." The dancers on the floor couldn't understand why the music was switched from a waltz to "Over the Rainbow" and in two seconds Judy was mobbed. The bandleader came down and said, "Judy, you better give them a treat or they won't let you alone." Judy sat on the table and in two seconds everything was quiet. Judy took the mic and sang "Over the

Rainbow" like she never sang it before. The crowd became so big that some of them had to sit on the floor. Judy lit up like an electric bulb. She seemed to be in seventh heaven while the crowd hollered, "More, Judy, more!"

Tully and I peeked in to see if she was still alive. When we saw how happy she was, we just put our hands up and said, "Thank God." But I motioned to Pupsenik and told him to keep his eye on Judy and see that she didn't get in any trouble as Tully and I were going up to our room.

As we were going up the elevator, I said, "Tully, there's a guy in this town who's a big meat packer and I understand that his slaughterhouse is about a block long so he must be up in the dough. I'm going to call him right now because when I met him in L.A., he sure was fond of me. I had him at my home a couple of times and one afternoon when I got home, there was a new Frigidaire and stove to match. That was his way of thanking me for giving him a good time."

I called his place of business and asked to speak to Oppie, which was short for Oppenheimer. He came to the phone and I said, "Oppie, this is Dottie. How would you like to show me the town?"

He said, "Where are you?" I told him and he said he would be there in half an hour. Well, he arrived and started reminiscing about all the people he had met at my place in Beverly Hills. He hadn't had his dinner yet so we ordered up a lot of goodies from the Pump Room. While we were having a nice rare steak and a couple of highballs, there was Judy in the doorway. I asked her what was wrong. Judy said she had a good dinner and sang a couple of numbers, but the mob got too big so she snuck out the back door. "My date didn't even know I left," she said. She took one look at Oppie and said, "Didn't I meet you somewhere before?"

Oppie said, "Yes, a couple of years ago at Dottie's house."

Judy said, "Oh yes, you're the Oppie that bought her the

Frigidaire and stove." Well, we all sat up until the wee hours of the morning and Oppie said he would pick me up and take me wherever I wanted to go in Chicago. I told him I wanted to see the house where I was born and then I wanted to see the little brick house that my mother and father owned when I was about six.

He said, "Give me a ring when you're ready and I'll be here to pick you up."

Dottie with Max H. Oppenheimer aka "Oppie."

The next morning, I met Oppie in front of the Ambassador East and he handed me a small box. I opened it and it was perfume, Chanel No. 5. He said, "See how I remember?"

Judy and Tully didn't like the idea of my leaving them behind but this was something I had to do by myself. I wanted to go back many years to my childhood days. We drove up to DeKoven Street where I was born. I closed my eyes and I could see myself playing ball and jacks on the sidewalk with my cousin Adele and all the kids. DeKoven Street was just a block away from where the Great Chicago Fire started with Mrs. O'Leary's cow, as the story had it. I sat there and just let myself dream. Oppie said, "Where do you want to go next?"

I said, "Okay, Oppie, let's go west now, to Douglas Park and our little red brick house that we moved to after DeKoven Street." He drove until we hit Troy Street and that's where the little brick house was. That used to be one of the finest neighborhoods in the city when I was a child but it had changed a lot.

Dottie and her brother Bernard with their grandfather
in front of their childhood home in Chicago.

After we had moved, Adele's folks rented the apartment next to us and we were together again. All of us kids went to the same school which was on the other end of the park. As the years went by, Adele acquired four sisters and a brother. As for me, I had two brothers to take care of.

My father, who was a cigar maker, only made $12.50 a week back then. Adele's father used to go from house to house until midnight, selling old and new clothes in order to keep his family together. And out of the $12.50 my father brought home, my mother managed to feed us and put a dollar away to help pay for the little red brick house.

I remember watching my father kiss two fingers on his hand and place them on a tin object nailed to the door. And I said, "Pa why do you always kiss this piece of tin when you come from work?"

My father said the piece of tin is called a *mezuzah*. "Every observant Jew that loves God has one of these on his door. This is for the day and the night I'm going to have with my family." He could tell by the smell when my mother was cooking and he would always thank God for the food we had. My mother enjoyed watching her husband and kids eat heartily, but she worried about the kids up the street who had nothing. She would drop some coins in a milk bottle whenever she could and at the end of the month, she would take this money to feed the family up the street. She called the milk bottle a *pushke*. Every observant Jew had a pushke in their kitchen to collect money for needy families. This was their way of thanking God for being fortunate enough to be able to feed their own family. Ma would put a little shawl over her head and run through the snow so that the little lady up the street and her five kids would have something hot to eat. My Ma and Pa were the salt of the earth.

I remember one night when we were kids, we had a terrific snowstorm and we could hear Adele's mother calling the family together, telling them dinner was ready. This night the storm was heavy and the blizzard was the worst we had ever seen. Everybody ran up the back stairs and before they opened the door, they shook the snow off their shoes and clothes. As they opened the door, the aroma from the food and the warmth that hit them made them let out cries of delight. By this time, there were seven people in the room and they were grabbing chairs to get around that table. On the stove there was a big pot of soup meat, about three or four pounds, and in this pot were also potatoes, carrots, string beans, and cabbage.

Now the meat cost about 30 cents and then they would throw in the liver or chicken necks or anything the butcher wanted to throw in and it wouldn't cost you anything extra. In the store there were also apples which were bruised and thrown into a barrel and when I came in and put my arms around Mr. Cohn and gave him a kiss on the cheek, he would say, "Alright, alright, that's enough—the apples are in the back." I would take a big bag and fill it up with apples and at home my mother would cut out the bad parts. Mr. Cohn was around 65 or 70 and he never had any children and I would try to give him the affection he never had. Well, we had apple pie for a month!

At Adele's place, her mother came out with a big fat herring on a platter. She sliced it thin, buttered slices of pumpernickel bread, put a slice of this herring on each square, and gave one to each person. Their mouths were watering before they even got the slices in. Adele's mother put the big pot of food in the middle of the table and everybody held up their plates to be filled. Everybody was humming a different tune; that room was full of love, contentment, and peace of mind.

Adele's mother was sucking on a soup bone which was full of marrow and she was hoping there would be some left for her husband who was coming in out of the cold that night. She managed to have a plate of leftovers in the oven for him. That meal didn't even come to a dollar but there were seven people who had their bellies full. When Adele's father came in out of the snow and her mother pulled those leftovers out of the oven, he was warm and happy in two minutes. He couldn't stop eating and finally said, "Do you know how lucky we are?"

When I was 13, my father died. I was the apple of my father's eye.

He wouldn't let anybody take care of him but me when he was dying of cancer, and I was with him every night. But on the night that my father died, my uncle had taken me to his house to get a good night's sleep. The next night, when I got home, I was walking past a glass door that led to the outside. Something made me walk over to this door and look outside—and there was my father, dressed in a white robe, kneeling, and throwing me a kiss, saying, "I love you." I pinched myself to see if I was awake, dead, or what. I turned around again and the form was gone. Could it have been my imagination or could it have been my dad saying good-bye since I wasn't with him at the last moment?

I knew I had to get a job because we had no money. I wasn't quite 14 yet so I asked a neighbor to sign an affidavit saying I was 15 in order to get a job at the Western Union Telegraph Company, picking up messages and putting them on file. That kept the family going in food as I had two brothers and a mother to take care of.

I knew I had to get something that paid more money. Adele landed a job at Sears and Roebuck's while I got a job in the basement of the Boston Store in downtown Chicago. I wasn't feeling too good but I didn't want anybody to know. When the house doctor examined me, he said I had to get out of that basement. I was transferred to the millinery French Room and for every $10 hat I sold, I made 90 cents. I was the youngest saleslady there—the other ladies had been on the floor for years and they were as old as Methuselah. I seemed to attract people to me and I was making money hand over fist. I would model the hats, giving them a nice song and dance. I worked there for a year or two to save up enough money for railroad fare to California.

As Oppie drove us up in front of the little brick house, a bunch of kids started crawling all over the car. I told Oppie I wanted to get out and that he should pick me up in half an hour. I walked over to the old wooden fence and looked up and down at this little brick house. It looked like a matchbox to me now but at one time, when I was little, it seemed like a big mansion.

I sat on the fence as if I were in a trance. I wondered if the big pepper tree was still in the backyard. I remembered my first skirt and shirtwaist with a patent leather belt around my hips, I thought I was the grandest thing in the Easter Parade. I remember the little Dutch band that played in the Pavilion in the park every Saturday night. We would have our dinner early so we could get good seats or some of the boys and girls would lie on the grass, bringing their dinners with them. All of us girls would buy these 50-cent white felt hats which had a band on it which read, "Oh you kid" and the park was filled with giant bushes of purple lilacs. Those were wonderful days but we were too young to appreciate it.

I remember one night, underneath the lighted lamppost, we played Run Sheep Run and my hand was caught on an iron picket fence and it started to bleed like a stuck pig. My friend Ralph, who later became a priest, said, "Keep your jaws working, Dottie, or you're liable to have lockjaw." Everybody gave me a stick of gum. I chewed on that gum all night long so my jaws wouldn't lock.

Just then, a little man came out from the house, interrupting my memories, and said, "Why are you crying?" I said, "I lived here 40 years ago and I was thinking about those wonderful days." He asked me if I would like to come inside. I said, "No. I'd like to go in the backyard" which I did, but the pepper tree was gone. No swings, no roses. It looked just like the rest of the neighborhood—run down and pretty dirty. I started to cry even harder. The little man must have thought I was out of my mind but I didn't care, I just sat there and cried. I looked up at the house and said, "Do you remember me and the good times we used to have here?" Just then, I saw Oppie pulling up. He looked at me and said, "What happened? Your eyes are red, your nose is running."

I said, "Oppie, I'm sad but I'm also happy."

He said, "You don't make sense." I looked back at the little brick house and it was like leaving a little child there all alone. Oppie said, "Come on, let's get back to your hotel. We can have lunch and you can put on a new face and forget all about the little brick house."

I said, "Oh no, Oppie. I'll never forget about that house. That's where I had my first date and everything was rosy even though I didn't know it at the time."

As we entered the hotel, Tully was downstairs. She took one look at me and said, "When you left, you looked beautiful. What in the hell happened to you?"

Oppie said, "Oh, she'll be fine as soon as she gets a new face on. She just turned the clock back quite a few years but I think it made her feel good." Then he said, "You girls figure out what you want to do tonight. I have to get back to my slaughterhouse. Ring me when you're ready."

When Tully and I got upstairs, Judy was dolling up for her date and she hollered, "Dottie, I think you're having a great time with Oppie—he sure is a hell of a guy. But Dottie, I'm going to have company tonight. Order a lot of flowers for my room and put some in the bathroom, too, and you two make yourselves scarce."

I told Tully, "You're going to come with me and Oppie tonight so don't worry about not having a date."

Tully said, "Why in the hell don't you grab this guy?"

I told her, "Well, you see, Tully, why is 'cause he's married! He doesn't live like it and he's been trying to get a divorce for the last two or three years but his wife said no. And why in the hell would she want to give up a meal ticket like that?"

"You know, Dottie, I think if you played your cards right, this guy would be yours, divorce or no divorce, because he seems to be so happy when he's with you," Tully said. "I heard him tell Judy that there isn't anything he wouldn't do for you."

"Well, Tully, he's got hot pants right now but we'll wait and see what happens in the next six months."

Judy was huffing and puffing, getting herself beautiful. She said, "I'm not leaving here tonight so don't you guys worry about me. I'm having everything brought up here, soft light and a good dinner and all the works." She looked like the cat that was about to swallow the canary.

I said, "I hope you know what you're doing." She was humming and singing as though she was back in her teenage years. I just figured this is the first round, let's see what happens.

Oppie took us to some of the finest places in Chicago. I never knew there were such places and I was born there. Oppie had brought a friend with him, hoping that Tully would like him, and Tully fell for him like a ton of bricks. He seemed to like Tully and Tully wasn't bad to look at. Tully whispered to me and said, "I hope he's not married."

Well, we painted the town red that night as we were all on cloud nine. I never saw Tully so full of fun as she was that night, it did my heart good. We didn't get home until daybreak. I peeked into Judy's room and all the lights were on. There was a note on the lamp which read, "When you guys get in, wake me up."

Tully said, "It's up to you, Dottie. I'm afraid to look in her bedroom." I opened the door and Judy was sound asleep with a little white poodle lying on the top of her head.

She opened her eyes and said, "You guys certainly deserted me tonight."

I said, "Didn't you tell us to make ourselves scarce?"

"How do you like my little guy?" Judy asked. He was the cutest little pup you ever saw—a little white ball of fuzz. Judy said, "I'm going to name him Tony and I'm going out to buy him a jeweled collar and he is going to New York with us. My date thought a lively little poodle would keep me company more than flowers. Let's all have breakfast together in the morning, so hit the hay, kids, and get some sleep."

"Oh, and one more thing," Judy said. "Tomorrow we all stay up here in this penthouse. No going out in the morning or evening. We are all going to rest up from this hilarious time we've been having or we'll never make it to New York. I know a lot of people in that town and we're going to hit all the shows and all the restaurants. And we're going to have even bigger flings there than we had in Chicago!"

Just then the phone rang and it was Oppie. I went to the phone and thanked him for the wonderful time he gave us and I told him we were leaving for New York the next day and that I wanted to say goodbye now. He asked me if there was anything I needed and told me he would see me in L.A. in a couple of months. Judy got up and started to do a soft-shoe dance with half her clothes off. She said, "I lost about five pounds and am I glad."

"This reminds me of the time I walked into Fred Astaire's dressing room without knocking when we were doing *Easter Parade* (1946). Do you remember that, Dot? When I saw how skinny he was and he had no toupee on his head, I decided then and there I was going to take him in hand and order his food for him. That's when you bawled me out and told me I had no business going into a man's dressing room without knocking because you could have seen a lot more than just his ribs."

"Do you know what I'm going to do with this poodle, Dottie?" Judy said. "The lady that's been cleaning for us here at the hotel has a little five-year-old girl. I'm going to give her this little dog. That will make her happy because I don't think we can take care of it in New York. Let's call her in right now and get it over with." The woman's name was Mary and when she came in the door, Judy held the pup up and said, "Would you like this dog for your little girl?" I never saw a person who could cry as fast as she did. She was so happy and said she would take good care of him and he would always have a good home. Judy picked up the little dog and kissed it right on the mouth and said goodbye.

We all felt a little sad when that little thing was carried out the door because he kept us in a happy mood, but after a couple of highballs we were all in the groove again. We had an early dinner as our train time was at 6:30 the next morning. At our table in the Pump Room there were decorations and a cake saying "Goodbye, Judy, Please Come Again." With the food they gave us that night, I think I put on five pounds. But Judy had said she lost five pounds and kept ordering highballs, knowing that Mr. Pupsenik would see that she got safely on the train. But she forgot about me, the little Indian who couldn't take firewater.

When we got to Union Station, there were two platforms, one where the trains were coming in and one where the trains were going out. As I got out of the car to walk toward the train, my legs began to wobble. I knew I wasn't steady. I was carrying Judy's jewel box and looking at the train that was coming in with all the servicemen. They were yelling at me and I was yelling back at them and I was waving the box and the three drawers opened up and the costume jewelry went flying through the air. Some of the guys were throwing their hats at me because they knew I was loaded and they were having fun. Every one of their faces looked like Mark, that husband of mine, who was lost in his plane. I could hear Judy hollering to Tully to get me on the train and not to worry about the jewelry because it's only costume.

Judy was pretty high herself but she could hold her liquor except when she got to giggling. As I got to the train I said, "Judy, I need to go to the toilet." Judy took me in and sat me down on the throne. I said, "Judy, are you mad at me?"

Judy laughed and said, "No, I'm not mad at you. I knew that last one was going to do it and it's really my fault." She said, "You sit there, Dottie. I'm going to order some coffee and tomato juice. I think we can all do with a little of that. Now you sit there until I get back or you're going to fall on your face."

There was a cabinet built right behind the toilet seat which held little books the size of the *Reader's Digest*. One of them fell out and landed on my shoulder and stayed there. I started to yell for Judy or Tully and when they came running I said, "Get this porter out of here! He's got his hand on my shoulder and he won't let me get up!" Well, Judy and Tully sat on the floor and laughed so hard that they became hysterical looking at the book that was on my shoulder. They made a beeline for the other bathroom and I thought the porter was still with me.

When they came back, Judy said, "Give me your right arm and pick up this little book that's on your shoulder. Now, you see? There's no hand and no porter in this room, it's all in that fuzzy mind of yours."

Well, the train took off and the sound of the whistle gave you a certain thrill. It was like being in a plane that just took off. Just then, there was a knock on the door and the porter said, "Is there anything you want, Miss Garland?" Judy said, "Yes, pull our beds down, please, and let's throw Dot in one of them."

Tully, who had been pretty quiet since the bathroom episode, suddenly said, "You know, I don't think anybody in their right mind would take a job with you two, yet I wouldn't give it up for all the tea in China. It's just like being on a merry-go-round. You never know what's coming next. Dottie sure is breathing heavy. When she gets up, I bet she'll be herself again." Then she said to Judy, "You sure think an awful lot of Dottie."

Judy said, "Why shouldn't I? She's gotten me out of more scrapes than you could count. You know she would defy anybody for me. I know I call her 'schnook' and 'Svengali'—I have more names for her than Carter's has pills, but I love her. So let's not make any more noise so she can get some sleep. I think that porter bit scared her."

Judy turned the radio on softly but I could hear "Slow Boat to China" starting to play and I sat right up in bed. I started to sway with the music and Judy started to sing. Tully just threw her hands up in the air and said, "Here we go again!" Judy called the porter to order some potato chips, tuna fish, and coffee. She then asked me how I felt. I said that I felt great.

The next morning, the William Morris office had one of their men waiting for us at the station and in about two minutes we were at the Carlyle Hotel. There was a suite of rooms for Judy and across the hall Tully and I also had a suite. As usual, the hotel had flowers and a big basket of fruit waiting. There wasn't anything we wanted that we couldn't get. Judy asked the bellboy if there was a chance he could get some corned beef sandwiches with garlic pickles at Rubin's for us. He said, "You bet! I'll be back in 20 minutes".

It turned out that Judy's picture, *The Pirate*, was playing at the Loew's State. We decided to go see it and Judy wanted to sneak up the back stairs so she wouldn't get noticed. I thought otherwise. When we were seated, I noticed we were just behind Earl Wilson. I asked Judy to bend over so I could whisper to her. "Judy, don't get scared but I'm going to cause a commotion here. Let your cape fall off your shoulders." She cooperated and the cape fell off. I said in a stage whisper, "Judy, pick up your cape."

As I had hoped, Earl Wilson heard me and turned around. His stage whisper was even louder than mine. "Hello Judy. How long are you going to be in town?" By now, people were craning their necks to get a look. The entire balcony started to hum. I could hear excited whispers of, "There's Judy!" coming from all around us, just as I had hoped. The hum spread and people started standing up to get a look. The entire balcony was in turmoil in less than five minutes. The ushers came up to tell everyone to be seated. Judy whispered in my ear, "Dottie, you're going to get me killed tonight."

I waved one of the ushers over. "I want you to stick close to Judy and Tully all the way down the stairs and protect Judy at any cost." I left them quickly after the picture was over, and, as the audience started streaming down the stairs into the large lobby, planted myself on a small platform off the balcony. As I saw Judy get halfway down the stairs, I yelled out, "Judy, Judy, wait for me!" At that point, the crowd practically carried Judy out to the street where the limousine was waiting. You never saw such excitement in your life. The crowd looked like an anthill overflowing! The street became black with people. Judy and Tully managed to get into the car. By the time I got to the car, there were five or six policemen on horseback trying to disperse the crowd. It was the wildest scene you have ever seen. I managed to get in the front seat with the chauffeur and he asked me if he should pull out. I told him to wait two more minutes.

By that time, Judy was screaming because the crowd was trying to lift the car. At that, I told the chauffeur to pull out but to take it easy since we were surrounded by a sea of people. The police officers worked frantically trying to keep the crowd back and when I turned around to look at Judy, she was as white as a ghost and so was Tully. We managed to get to the hotel safely. When we got upstairs, we could hear Judy's knees knocking. She drank a small glass of bourbon and calmed down. She looked at me and said, "Okay, Svengali. Do you want my blood?"

"Well, Judy," I replied, "You're going to make all the headlines tomorrow. You're going to get a million dollars worth of publicity after the stunt I pulled tonight." Sure enough, when we got the morning papers, the headlines screamed out the story. It had been Judy's night. New York had never seen anything like that before. The phone was ringing off the hook. Everybody was calling after reading the story. We not only got a million dollars worth of publicity but we shocked the whole country. Everybody wanted to know if Judy was still alive after that cloudburst. We all stayed in the hotel that day. In fact, we were afraid to go out. That didn't last too long, however.

While we were in New York, Judy got a crush on a songwriter who was writing some tunes for a Broadway show. He was married and his wife was just as feisty as Judy was. He kept telling the wife he was working nights while he was seeing Judy. Judy sensed that this dame was going to give her trouble.

One night, when they were having dinner, there was a knock at the door of our hotel room. It was the wife looking for her missing husband. It was a good thing that Tully and I hadn't left yet. Judy grabbed her date and put him in the shower and told him to stay in the corner of the shower so he wouldn't get too wet, after turning on the water!

His wife looked around and said, "I guess I must have the wrong suite." When she closed the door, Judy ran back to the bathroom and when he stepped out, he looked like a wet fish.

He said, "Call me a cab, Judy, and I'll go home and put on some dry clothes while she's looking for me. I'll be back in an hour. Hold the fort for me, Judy." They were like two kids in a sandbox. Tully and I took off for 42nd Street leaving Judy laughing thinking that she put one over. Judy enjoyed herself that week.

Another night in New York, Judy came waltzing in at about 3:30 in the morning and found me sitting in a chair holding a long stick. "Don't you know there are telephones in New York?" I yelled. Judy told me later that she wanted to slam the door on me but was afraid to so thought we might as well get it over with.

"The studio has been calling," I said, "Vincente has been calling, and I couldn't tell them where you were. The only thing I could say was that you were out on the town having fun."

"Alright, I'll tell you where I was so I can go to sleep. There is a nightclub across the river and there was an entertainer there that everyone was talking about and saying how great he was. So I wanted to see for myself. When I got there, I never saw such a wild bunch of people. There was Billy Daniels singing to the crowd. You never heard such a commotion. When he saw me, he had the band stop playing and yelled to me to come on up. Before the night was over, I think Billy and I sang every song that was written in the last 25 years. The next thing I knew, Billy and I were dancing on the floor."

As Judy Garland's career at MGM was winding down, Dottie worked with her on several more classics: *Easter Parade* (1948), *Words and Music* (1948), and, as seen here, *In the Good Old Summertime* (1949) with Van Johnson. Next to Dottie is Judy's hairdresser Betty Pedretti.

When we got back to town, Judy's time at MGM was coming to an end, but we didn't know it. I remember when we were working on *Summer Stock*, the picture that turned out to be Judy's last one at MGM. Gene Kelly, Judy, and I left the back lot walking slowly toward Judy's dressing room. You'd think the world was on our shoulders we had worked so hard that day. Judy was hoping that Tully would have sandwiches and cold drinks for us to pump a little life into us, but there was no Tully. Gene threw himself into an easy chair, and Judy on a blue satin spread across her bed. I threw myself across the foot of the bed as my day was pretty tough keeping the perspiration off of Judy—she had worked so hard that day.

Summer Stock was a hard picture which seemed to take the life out of all of us. The room was so quiet you could hear the petal of a rose drop. All of a sudden, Judy asked me if I believed in God. It took me by surprise. I stopped for a moment and said, "Yes Judy, I believe in God, but I don't know what God is. God may be a great power that hovers over all of us, who keeps the oceans in their place so they can't swallow all the land; who puts the millions of colors in the flowers, who gives us the trees, who gives the food out of the ground. God gives us a million things that we take for granted. I don't know, but I believe."

Just then, the door opened and in walked Tully with the sandwiches and cold drinks. After wolfing those down, we felt we were alive again. Judy asked Gene to practice one more hour on a particularly hard step and after an hour Judy had it down. Gene had a big grin and Judy said, "God or no God, he sure worked the pants off of me today."

Just then, we were called to the set and Judy started clowning with Gene Kelly. Gene handed her a bottle of Coca-Cola and a chocolate bar. He said, "This will give you the energy you'll need for the rest of the afternoon."

While they were munching on a chocolate bar, in walked Frank

Sinatra. And from then on, the director couldn't handle any of them. The clowning that went on was unbelievable! Those three monkeys had everybody hysterical. A few minutes later, in walked Peter Lawford and the fun began all over again.

Judy enjoyed doing *Summer Stock* because we had all kinds of animals and a farm built on the back lot and also because she had something to run home to—Liza would be waiting for us. As I practically lived up there with Judy and Vincente back then, you'd think I was Judy's mother and Liza's grandmother.

As we got into the house that night, the governess stopped us and said she had just put Liza to sleep and we couldn't go down into the nursery. This governess was so crazy about Liza, she became overpowering. She felt like Liza was her child and Judy sensed it. She turned to Minnelli and said, "We've got to get rid of this dame." Vincente, knowing how wonderful this woman was with Liza, tried to talk Judy out of it, but Judy said, "Pay her off and get her out of here tonight." Judy went to the phone and called the part-time nurse to take a steady job with Liza, as Liza liked her and so did Judy.

You can bet your bottom dollar that Vincente gave the poor governess a check and probably a big bonus and sent her packing. I think Judy would have kicked me and Vincente out the front door along with the governess if she did not have her way.

After the woman was gone, Judy said, "How about some food?" Pearl, her cook who heard her, said, "Steak, baked potatoes and sour cream, and Caesar salad coming up." Judy said, "Let it come, and bring a couple of highballs, too," and we were on cloud nine.

When Pearl came up to take the dirty dishes, she said, "You guys did okay." Judy said, "You would think we were in a POW camp and this was our last meal!" and this made Pearl feel good. To know Pearl was to love her. She was everything rolled up in one. After a good meal and a couple of highballs, Judy sat on the sofa in front of the fireplace and her head started to nod and she went into a little snooze which had never happened before.

Vincente motioned to me to not say anything, to see what would happen when she opened her eyes because Judy and sleep were the worst of enemies. Vincente and I went out on the porch, which overlooked the Valley on one side and Los Angeles on the other, and the blue and red lights that glittered looked like diamonds in the rough. People who fly in on an airplane say this view of southern California is the most beautiful sight to see, but it had nothing on the view from the Minnelli home.

Just then, we heard Judy say, "Where did everybody go?" Judy joined us on the porch and said, "Gee, I feel good, let's have a couple more highballs." Vincente said, "Let's go easy because you have a rough day tomorrow. You're rehearsing your dancing with Gene and you know what a perfectionist he is." But Judy grabbed hold of Vincente and said, "Vin-chent-ay," which means Vincente in Italian, "Let's have some fun tonight." Whenever she wanted to get on the good side of Vince, she would call him "Vin-chent-ay."

Chuck Walters was directing *Summer Stock* and we would have to be there on time as there was no fooling around with him. Joe Pasternak was the producer of this picture and he loved Judy very much. Vince had just finished fixing a shaker of highballs. Judy said, "Okay, Vincente, you and Dottie have one with me."

The air was warm on the porch and there was a full moon glittering among the stars. Pearl had fixed a couple of bowls of popcorn and peanuts and we kept munching on them. Judy had two highballs to my one. I said, "This is it, Judy, No more for me." Judy turned around and said, "Aw, come on Dottie, don't be chicken." Vincente sat back in a big easy chair, getting a big kick out of the both of us. I took one more highball and that one turned me into a rubber-ding-dong.

I started to get up from the porch to walk into the living room. Instead of my feet going down to the floor, the floor was coming up to my feet; everything in the room seemed to be spinning, and I said, "Judy, I don't feel good." Judy had two sofas, one on each side of her fireplace. She managed to get me on one while she sat on the other, laughing so hard the tears ran down her cheek.

Vincente asked Pearl to bring up some black coffee, thinking it would ease me down a bit. Pearl took me in her arms and put my head on her bosom, and these bosoms were big as all outdoors. She said, "Dottie, why do you do this when you know you can't drink?" I took a big sigh and said, "Pearl, it feels so good to tell the world to go bugger off."

Within a few minutes, I dozed off to sleep, and Judy woke me and said, "Get into these pajamas. You can sleep on this couch and I'll sleep on the other." I said, "Oh no, you won't. Get in there with Vincente. It's midnight, and we all need to get some sleep." Lights went out, everything was quiet.

Later on that night, I must have hit the bathroom, but coming back, I couldn't find the front of the couch. I landed on the floor, behind the couch, with my arms holding on. I could hear Judy's bedroom door opening up and hear her say, "Vincente, you want to see something funny? Get a load of what's on the floor."

And I said, "Judy, never let me have that second or third drink because I'm like an Indian with firewater." Judy kissed me on the cheek and said, "Oh, Dottie, I love you so much."

Pearl got us up an hour earlier than we planned the next morning. She was afraid we wouldn't be on the ball. I got Judy made up just beautiful and we were at the studio on time. Judy got into her clothes on the set, as we had 200 extras working that day. To look at us, you would never know the fun we had the night before. And you'd certainly never know that all those years at MGM were about to come to an end.

5.

Leaving MGM and Heading to Europe with Judy and Sid

There is a time in my life I'll always remember. That's when I took Judy's place at the dinner table every night with Vincente and Liza while Judy was playing hanky-panky at the Beverly Hills Hotel with Sid Luft. I would no sooner get home from the studio when the telephone would be ringing and it would be Pearl on the other end saying, "You have 15 minutes to get here. Dinner is about ready." Pearl would entice me with a wonderful dinner just so it wouldn't be so lonesome for Liza and Vincente. I would give them a lot of talk about what happened at the studio that day, jokes just to keep the ball rolling, otherwise you would feel a streak of loneliness there. Vincente would always have a sterling silver candelabra on the table which held six candles. This added a touch of glamour to the table. The gardenias would just touch it up. I couldn't say no to these two because I could feel the heaviness in the house without Judy.

We turned on the music in the living room and I started to dance with Liza right behind me. Vincente would look up from a script he was reading and get a couple of chuckles out of Liza and me. I was getting pretty tired and wanted to get home when I learned I had been elected to take Liza to a movie. When I got to the house the next day, Liza was splashing in the pool with Barry Sullivan's little girl; the higher the splash, the louder the laughter. Pearl came out with terrycloth robes and put them on the two girls and gave them each a sandwich and a Coke and before I knew it, Liza was dressed and in my car and off we went. Well, I got her in the theater but damned if I could get her out. She was just as bullheaded as her mother. She wanted to stay for another showing and I told her if she wanted to stay she'd be staying alone because I was going back to her house to have dinner with her daddy. The next thing I knew she was running up the aisle after me saying, "Dottie, Dottie, wait for me!" When we got back to the house, there was Vincente outside with a long face and there was Pearl right behind him. I never saw anybody as frightened as they were but relieved when they saw us.

When Judy and I were leaving the studio one night while working on *Annie Get Your Gun* (1950), I noticed she went into a cold chill. She said, "Dottie, take me to the Minnelli house. I don't want to go to the Beverly Hills Hotel where Sid is waiting for me. I'm sick and I don't know what it is."

I drove her up the hill where Pearl was waiting. She took one look at Judy and said, "What's wrong with my baby?" Judy could hardly make it to the bed. Judy was sick but nobody would buy it. She had hollered wolf too many times and now nobody would believe her but Pearl and I knew this was the real thing.

Vincente was glad to see Judy home as he knew Pearl would take care of her. Liza kept coming in and out of the room which made Judy feel good. She turned to me and said, "Why am I running away from all this? What's wrong with me?" But knowing Judy as I did, as soon as she was back on her feet she would be back with Sid Luft again. That phone never stopped ringing. When the executives learned that

Judy couldn't report in the next morning, they thought it was another gag of hers but if Judy's life depended on it, she couldn't even crawl to the studio, she was that sick. She had a bad case of the flu.

Joan Blondell visiting the *Annie Get Your Gun* (1950) set with Dottie and Judy. Suffering from overwork and exhaustion, Garland was replaced after two months with Betty Hutton. She was nearing the end of her time at MGM.

That afternoon, Judy's living room was full of men who came up to tell her she was fired—for real, this time. There were the lawyers from the studio, the business managers, the producers, and every one of these guys was fighting with each other. All of a sudden, in walked the efficiency man who does all the dirty work. He said, "Judy is no longer with MGM. Her contract is broken and she is being replaced by Betty Hutton in the film." This man was hard as nails. He was backed up by the bankers who controlled the money.

Judy was heartbroken and couldn't believe it. She started to cry and said, "Can they do that to me?" I said, "Yes, there is a clause in every contract favoring the studio."

"After all, Dottie, look at all the money I made for them over the years. I'll make them sorry for this."

Pearl took over and I went home. By this time, I needed a couple of aspirins. I went to bed hoping for a good night's sleep. At about two in the morning, the phone rang. It was some reporter asking me if it was true that Judy had just cut her throat. How he got my number I'll never know. I was dressed in about two minutes, got in my car, and started for the Minnelli house. When I got there, I never saw so many cars in my life. I managed to get into the house and found Judy locked in her bedroom so nobody could see her. I took one look at her and there wasn't even a scratch on her neck but we had to keep that from the reporters outside and when they left, they didn't know whether she had done it or not.

After a week, Judy was on her feet again and as much as she had sometimes hated going through the MGM gates, she missed it. She said, "Dottie, MGM was my second home. What am I going to do now?"

Judy started going out again every night to meet up with Sid. I wondered how much Vincente was going to take. I knew Judy was going to have to make up her mind whether it was Vincente or Sid because this couldn't go on much longer. She talked her plans over with Sid and he advised her to take a contract offer from the London Palladium. With no check coming in from MGM, Judy had to get money from somewhere because Judy never saved her money. She wanted Tully to get in touch with Buddy Pepper who she wanted as her pianist on the concert tour. He was also a songwriter, his biggest song was probably "Vaya con Dios." In fact, Buddy was the first date Judy had when she was around 14. Buddy agreed and got all of her music together. Then we had to get shots and our passport pictures and when Tully and I saw our pictures, we thought we looked like Dracula's mother.

The next thing was where to get some money. Judy sold what bonds she had and the bank gave her a chunk of money on her Palladium contract. Then there were clothes we had to buy for Judy and get her decked out so she could take London by storm.

The following week, we found ourselves in Chicago again and from Chicago to New York. Sid said he would meet us in London so Buddy, Tully, Judy, and I headed overseas. When we got there, we stayed at the Dorchester Hotel. That was a stone's throw from the Palace and Hyde Park. Buddy had his room, Tully and I had a suite of rooms, and Sid and Judy were on the same floor. We went down to the Palladium and got all our music together and rehearsed with the orchestra.

To our surprise, Danny Kaye was in town. He was to follow Judy at the Palladium when her engagement was up. Judy worked awfully hard rehearsing for the opening night and when that night came, the crowd was around the block about four deep. They had these large posters of Judy outside the theater. All the seats were sold out.

Judy packed that house to standing room capacity. I never saw her work so hard and the crowds just became bigger and bigger. The second week Judy became a little lax and said, "Dottie, sit up in that box close to the stage and use that small megaphone and keep me on my toes."

I would sit in this box every night—in the back of it so the audience couldn't see me but so Judy could hear me. I would holler, "Let 'em have it, Judy! Louder, Judy! Fire up, Judy!"

Judy would blast out as though somebody just gave her a shot in the arm. On some of the nights Danny Kaye would sit in the box with me and say, "Boy, she sure is great."

There was a critic who came to the Palladium every night. He was on the scale of Earl Wilson in New York, only he was tougher than Earl. Well, this guy gave me headlines in the London paper saying, "When you go in to see Judy Garland, notice the girl in the box who keeps Judy going." He came up the back stairs to the box to see what I looked like. This critic took a liking to me and he and his wife asked me out to dinner. Judy told me to go but Sid was madder than hell on account of the write-ups I got in the London papers.

Bob Hope was in town and came to the show. So did Marilyn Maxwell and many other celebrities. We all went to a party given by the owner of the Palladium and was it a plush place—all in red velvet. The band played and everybody was dancing. Everybody was happy as a lark. The food was great but Judy was wondering where Sid was. He was gallivanting around London, getting tailor-made suits and specially made shoes of Italian leather. Boy, that guy had a wardrobe second only to the King. Judy was sure mad when he didn't show up. I said, "Forget it, he will pop in any minute now." He did, and when he saw how mad Judy was, he started flirting with some other girl and that got Judy wild. Judy picked up a bottle and I thought she was going to hit him over the head with it but Buddy Pepper picked her up and made her dance with him and before I knew it, Sid and Judy were dancing on the floor together. The crowd was going to another nightspot in London. Tully and I asked to be driven back to the Dorchester Hotel because we had had it. We wanted to get a good night's sleep.

I was sound asleep, flat on my back the length of the bed with my covers over me. As I lay there on my back, I felt somebody on top of me breathing in my face, holding my shoulders down and saying that four-letter word which I hate. It's not the word you think it is, it's even worse. Judy told this character that this is the only four-letter word that I never use so he kept saying it over and over in my ear and I couldn't move. I could hear voices over in the corner of the dark room trying to muzzle their laughs with their hands over their mouths. It was Sid and Judy. Tully got up and turned on the light and said she'd had enough of this craziness and lo and behold, when she turned on the light and I saw who was on top of me, it was none other than that wonderful guy called Danny Kaye. He was so full of laughs and jokes that we stayed up until daylight.

Judy had to get some sleep because she had to satisfy her audience that night so Tully kicked them all out of the room. At about five in the afternoon, we all started for the Palladium so Judy could rehearse a few numbers. The crowds were tremendous at the stage door trying to get an autograph from Judy. Judy signed as many as she could. Buddy Pepper was at the piano, rehearsing with the orchestra. Judy was singing loud and clear, everything seemed to go wonderfully until later that night.

Before the show, Judy had said to me, "Dottie, I feel wobbly tonight."

I said, "Judy, if anything should happen, laugh it up, make a big joke of it."

When Judy walked out on the stage, I felt she wasn't steady on those high heels of hers but she was fine for the first half of the show. Then when she started the second half, she put her arms out and said, "Hi, everybody," and with that, she went right down on her fanny in the middle of the stage.

The audience rose to its feet and Buddy Pepper left the piano and ran to pick her up. She had one shoe on and one shoe off. Buddy got her up and Judy turned to the audience and said, "I'll throw my shoes to the wind and sing till the cows come home!" The audience whistled, applauded, and shouted, "Sing, Judy, sing!" Judy walked to the edge of the stage, sat down, and let her feet dangle over the edge, and she sang that night until her throat was raw. I think she sang every song she knew. The audience showed its appreciation by banging on their seats, whistling, and yelling, "Judy! Judy!" Danny

Kaye was there that night and he said only Judy could hold a mob like this in the palm of her hand. Sid wasn't there, he was out on the town. He missed it that night and what a show it was. Everybody heard about Judy's fall. It even reached L.A. We got more telegrams and calls asking what went on.

I remember when we were all in Judy's dressing room at the Palladium. There was a knock at the door and in walked Bogie, Lauren Bacall, and Katharine Hepburn. Kate and Bogie were on their way to do *The African Queen* (1951) and Bacall was going along with them. The thing that took my eye was the mink coat that Lauren Bacall was wearing. It was the most magnificent mink I had ever seen. She opened it up and said, "Look, Judy, I'm pregnant." She patted her stomach and said, "Whatever it is, it's kicking its way to stardom." I knew Hepburn from MGM. Kate motioned to me to come over. She explained the picture to me and wanted pointers on what make-up she should use. I made a chart for her and I think she followed up on it as she was very anxious to get my opinion.

We had a couple more weeks on this engagement and then we took some time to see London as the tourists see it. The first thing we did was to go to the Tower of London where all the Crown Jewels were on display. At noon, they would shoot off a cannon from the top of the Tower but we didn't know that was coming and it damn near broke our eardrums! Judy kept complaining about her ear. Tully couldn't hear for two days and I swore I'd never go back to that place again if they gave it to me. Judy said she could hear that goddamn cannon noise for two weeks after.

From there we went to Eton College which is supposed to be the most famous college in the world. Of course, they wouldn't let us in. We went into the courtyard behind the college and in this courtyard there were slabs of cement about seven or eight feet long and about four feet wide. These slabs would tell you who was buried there. You had to be somebody big to be buried there—a king, queen, or a sir. Judy jumped from one of these slabs to the other. It looked like she was playing hopscotch. I said, "Judy, stop it. They're liable to throw us out of here." Judy said, "I just want to let 'em know I'm in town!"

From there we went to Windsor Castle which was out toward the country and that summer castle was for royalty only. It was a beautiful sight to see. Well, we took in a lot of places in London but the following week we decided to go to Scotland. We were in Edinburgh, Scotland, and our hotel was facing the castle on the hill where Mary, Queen of Scots, was beheaded. We got into the castle and climbed all the stairs to the tower and as we climbed up we could see blood stains on every step. Now these blood stains could not be real after these many hundreds of years, but this was a good come-on for tourists.

Sid and Judy went on a buying spree in Scotland. Sid came back with some wonderful sweaters that you could only buy in Scotland and a set of new golf clubs in a gold bag that was made of leather. We all felt like we wanted to go back to London and the Dorchester Hotel.

Buddy Pepper was sitting in my room when we got there. He had a long face on him and I said, "What's bothering you?"

He said, "I haven't had a check for two weeks."

Tully spoke up and said, "Neither have I. Let's find out who is stopping our checks."

Buddy said, "It's alright for you two because you're on Judy's bill."

I said, "Okay, when mealtime comes, you head to our room and be on our bill, too. We'll order three meals instead of two. That will at least give you food until this thing is settled."

I told Judy about this and she told me I was doing the right thing. "You sneak Buddy into your room and whenever you order, order for Buddy, too." Oh boy, did we order. By this time, Sid had appointed himself Judy's manager and I didn't think any of us would get another paycheck.

I said, "Judy, where is all the money you made? Do you have any of it at all? Tully and I would like to take a plane to Paris while we're on this side of the ocean because we'll probably never get another chance."

Judy said, "All my money is in an attache case that is tied to Sid's wrist, but don't worry, we're all going over to Paris for a couple of weeks. I've already arranged that."

I could sense that Sid didn't like me and what I was doing by putting Judy wise to what was going on. Judy said, "I know what he's doing, Dottie, but I love the guy. It's only money and if you don't shut up, he'll send you home in a row boat." Judy was so crazy about this guy that anything he did she would ask for more. Sometimes I think he had her hypnotized.

The next night, Tully and I went up to our room to order dinner and we snuck Buddy in so he could have some, too. After dinner, Judy came to me and said, "I've got something to tell you. I'm going to marry Sid."

I said, "How in the hell can you be married to two men at the same time?"

"Well, Dottie, we'll cross that bridge when we get to it."

Oh dear God, here we go again.

The following week, Judy had some time off and we went to Paris. We stayed at the Hotel de Crillon which was right next door to the American Embassy and on the corner where the Champs-Elysées Boulevard started. We looked out of our window at some great big beautiful waterways and fountains going as high as you could see. This was the corner where Marie Antoinette was beheaded.

I said, "Judy, there's one place I want to go and that's the streets of old Montmartre and the hill where Maurice Chevalier's mother lives. That's the street where St. Peter's Church is high on the hill. Chevalier told me once that his mother never missed a morning going into that famous church. He told me about his mother and how much he loved her."

"I also want to see the Flea Markets and the flower markets. There are so many things to see here in Paris. I want to see Napoleon's Tomb, I want to go to Notre Dame, and I'm also going to get into that famous opera house that Paris is noted for."

Judy said, "Shut up, Dot, I want to tell you about the places I want to see. I want to go to the Louvre. I want to see the Tuileries. I want to see the waxworks. That place is enough to give you the heebie-jeebies and if you don't stop fighting with Sid, he'll have you waxed up. We'll start tomorrow."

I said, "Oh no, I'm starting tonight! I'm going up the street to the hills of Montmartre at night when it's all lit up. Paris is most beautiful at night and I'm going to dress up like a real Parisian."

Well, I did, and was approached by two or three guys. The only word I knew in French was "Oui" which was something I should never have said. Before I knew it, I had a couple of arms around my waist but to my amazement, I heard somebody say, "How are you doing, Dot?" It was Tully and Buddy, following me under Judy's orders and boy, was I glad to see them as I think I would have been accosted right then and there. Tully said, "This should only happen to me!"

The three of us started out for one of those French cafes. We managed to get in but the only thing we ordered was a bottle of wine because we didn't have much money. Buddy said, "To be in Paris without a dime in your pocket is pretty lousy. What can we do about it? Use your head, Dot."

"Well, kids," I said. "I've got news for you. There are some shows Judy wants to see and when I told Judy how expensive they are, she said she'd get the money from Sid while he sleeps."

About three in the morning, Judy knocked on our door. She had two rolls of bills in her hands, big enough to choke a horse. To us, these bills looked like painted cigar coupons—the kind we had back home, but they were real money. None of us realized how much money it was.

Judy doled out some to Tully and some to Buddy. She gave me most of it. I threw mine in the bottom of my overnight bag. The next day, Tully and I took off to see everything that was possible to see. We walked all over Paris. My feet were so swollen I didn't know if I had my shoes on or off but we kept on going until we hit Notre Dame. I couldn't stand the pain in my feet any longer so I took my shoes off, put them under my arm, put a handkerchief on my head, and we went in. We stayed there for about an hour but I could have stayed there all night. Being there gave you a sense of belonging to someone up there. I could feel myself sitting right in the palm of His hand. It gave me a cool, clean feeling, even to the tune of loving Sid.

Well, I couldn't get my shoes back on so I walked through the streets of Paris in my stocking feet. I figured nobody knew me so what did I care? When I got back to the hotel, my feet were practically blistered and who was waiting for me? None other than Her Highness, Judy. She said, "You guys are really seeing Paris and I'm not seeing anything." She was kind of pitying herself and I didn't go along with it.

I said, "You want Sid and he wants to count your money, and if you keep this up neither one of you will see Paris."

Judy said, "Alright, buster, tomorrow is my day with you. We're going to take a bus, we're going to ride up and down the Eiffel Tower, we're going to the Palace of Versailles, and after that we're going to a sidewalk cafe and sit ourselves down and watch the Parisians going by."

The next day at the café, we were talking about the little trap doors we saw in the bedrooms at the Palace of Versailles, I guess the kings and dukes and what-have-yous used to get down on their bellies and crawl through these little trap doors and visit whatever lady they wanted to without being watched. Boy, there was plenty of hanky-panky going on in those days!

As we were sipping our coffee, two guys walked up to our table and said, "Hello, Judy. Do you mind if we sit down with you?"

Judy said, "No, pull up a chair." They were a couple of reporters from a Parisian newspaper.

They said, "How do you like our Paris?"

Judy said, "We were just talking about the pink marble castle that one of the kings built for Marie Antoinette and that black coach of hers is sure well preserved. They should put a coin machine outside that castle and I'm sure the tourists would have paid for this site over and over again."

One reporter said, "You Americans have an eye for money but we take it away from you. Have you seen the new Paris built with money from the Marshall Plan? Those big apartments and hotels and bridges? You people don't know how to hold on to your money. There isn't a country that doesn't take it away from you."

By this time, Judy was kicking my shins under the table. I knew what that meant but I couldn't keep my mouth shut after that remark. I said, "You ought to be glad that the Americans are a bunch of dummies. Some day we'll get wise and tell all of you to go bugger off. Too bad we haven't got a White House full of Teddy Roosevelts. He would take that big stick and ram it up where it belongs."

Judy leaned over and whispered in my ear. "If you don't shut up, they're liable to throw you in the Bastille."

Both of the men started to laugh and said, "You know, Judy, she should be President of the United States."

I said, "If I was, you people wouldn't have all these bridges and finery. I would see that our people wouldn't go to bed hungry and they wouldn't be taxed where they could hardly breathe. It's pretty hard to see our tax money poured down the sewers of every country and have them all laugh back at us."

Judy and I started back for the hotel leaving these two newspaper characters still sipping their coffee. What I would have loved to have done was to kick both of them in their you-know-whats.

When Judy and I were in Paris, we had shrimp at some restaurant with a sauce that was equal to none. Judy kept raving about it and said, "Dottie, I'll be right back." Well, I sat there about 45 minutes and no Judy. I became alarmed and went to the ladies room to see if she was there. I damn near walked into the men's room thinking she might have gone through the wrong door. The Maître D' saw me looking around and asked if I was looking for Judy. I said yes and he told me to go to the main kitchen. I opened the door and there was Judy, sitting on a high stool with a yellow bowl in her lap and that delicious dressing just oozing out of her mouth. The more she ate, the more the chef put into the bowl and that night she got sick as a dog. From that night on, Judy never went looking for recipes. She had had her fill with the shrimp.

The next thing we knew, we were faced with Sid Luft who was about to question us about the money. Judy put her finger up to her lips as if to say to me, "Shh... don't talk."

Sid asked us if we had been in his room last night. We shook our heads no. "Well, somebody was. I'm about ten thousand dollars short."

Judy laughed and said, "You know, Sid, I think you got your zeros wrong."

Sid said, "I better have or there's going to be trouble around here."

That night, we were afraid Sid was going to search our room so I took the money and put it in my girdle and slept in my girdle all night.

"Judy, Tully and I are going to get the hell out of here. We're going to take a plane to Rome. We'll be back tomorrow night. You really don't need us and Sid doesn't want us hanging around anyway."

Judy got a scared look on her face and said, "My God, if anything happens to the two of you, what am I going to do? I'm scared. Don't go."

"Don't be chicken. Nothing will happen to us and we'll have a wonderful time. Just think of all the money I got in my girdle!"

Tully and I packed an overnight bag, went across the Champs-Elysées to the travel agency, and bought two tickets to Rome. When we got on the plane, we thought we'd never reach Rome because the plane was like an old wooden crate, swaying with the wind. But we landed and we went to a hotel high on a hill that seemed to be made out of marble. The floors were marble and the walls were marble and there were fantastic chandeliers made of crystal. Tully said, "This is too rich for our blood. I don't think we have enough money for this place."

I said, "Don't forget the roll of bills I've got on me and the money Judy gave you. We're really going to live it up here. First place we go is the Vatican. From there we're going to the old Coliseum. I understand all the poor people are taking the bricks out of the walls. Pretty soon there won't be a Coliseum for the tourists to see. I want us to take a drive down the famous Appian Way and then go down under the street to the catacombs where all those priests were killed."

As we were walking up the street, somebody pinched me in the you-know-where. I was ready to hit him with my purse but he stood there grinning and said, "You American?" I said yes, ready to kill him.

He pointed to an old taxi and said, "You want to see Rome? I take you."

For the next five hours, he took us all over Rome and to some tiny hole-in-the-wall places to eat. We had spaghetti coming out of our ears. We asked him to give us another five hours the next day. This guy was priceless—he was so much fun. I decided that he could pinch me anytime he wanted to.

When we got to the hotel, Tully said, "Let's call Judy and tell her we're staying over another day. I'm sure it will be okay with her as long as she has her lover boy. I'm sure if it was up to him, he'd let us stay a week."

After seeing Rome, we went down to pay the bill. Tully was worried that we wouldn't have enough money. She said, "Where's the roll of bills Judy gave you?" I fished it out and handed it to the man at the front desk. I told him to take what we owed him. His eyes opened wide and he called the manager. They both looked at us as though we were two thieves.

The manager said, "Where did you get all this money?"

I turned to Tully and said, "I think we're in trouble."

We explained to him that we were working for Judy Garland who was in Paris and had given us this money to see Rome. He happened to be one of Judy's fans and he damn near put the red carpet out for us. He took the money out of the roll of bills I handed him. He looked back at us and said, "Do you girls know how much money there is here? You have not only enough to pay your bill, you have enough to buy this place!"

I turned to Tully and said, "Sid was right. Judy better get this money back into his case without him knowing it. How she'll do it we'll never know but she will."

We got on a plane that night and were soon back in Paris. I went to Judy and said, "Get this money back into Sid's case. There's over ten thousand dollars here. Sid was right about the zeros. Give him knockout drops or get him drunk or get him in bed but get this money back there!"

Judy said, "Stop worrying and leave it to me." She managed it somehow and Sid was never the wiser. I'm so grateful to Judy for that fun adventure. How in the world could a dame like me ever afford a European trip like that?

One of the highlights of my life was a ride I took down the

Seine. I got up early one morning and left everybody sleeping, and I tiptoed out of the hotel to take the first ride down the Parisian river. When I got there, I found out I wasn't the only one as there were quite a few waiting for the first boat ride. They were all carrying bags of food which they intended to eat as the day went on. I got myself seated comfortably with my arms stretched out over the top of my seat. I bent my body back and as we took off the mist of the water hit my face and it was so cool and refreshing and I could only think of the song Fred Astaire sang about "Heaven, I'm in Heaven."

Just then, a bag came over my head and into my lap. As I looked up, I saw a Frenchman about 70 years old who looked like an aristocrat. He said in his thick French accent that he noticed I didn't have a bag of food with me like the others. By that time, he was sitting on my right and I said to myself here we go again but that wasn't the case. He just wanted company and as we rode down the river, he told me fairy tales about France I don't think anybody ever heard before. I was hoping he would never stop. As the sun went down and the ride was over, he said he was going to take me to where the poor French people enjoy life. As we approached a café, you could hear the accordions, it was like something out of a movie. As he opened the door, I felt like I was in a painting by Toulouse-Lautrec.

The men in the café had little colored handkerchiefs around their necks and they wore little berets. Half of them had their arms around their women who were robust gals who looked like they could make any man happy. Everyone had their wine glasses filled to the brim and the tables were filled with goodies. Most men had roasted chicken hanging out of their mouths with wine in one hand and were patting other women's behinds as they passed by with their other hand.

The next thing I knew, the Frenchman sat me down at a table and ordered food for the both of us. It seemed like everybody knew him. When they brought me my food, it was a piece of meat which was about an inch and a half thick. This piece of meat was done up in wine sauce and it was covered in burnt almonds and the trimmings that went with it were fit for a king.

I don't think I was ever as happy as I was that night. It was about 2:00 am when I realized I should get back to the hotel but he said no, he wanted me to see some of the canvasses he painted. I thought to myself, what can I lose? I never realized how much of an artist he was so I went and I thought if worse comes to worse and I had to fight this guy off, I would scare him by saying yes. But it never came to that. His apartment looked over the Seine and he had about a hundred paintings that were to be sold. He told me to pick out any one that I liked. I picked a painting of the river and the flowering trees. I had no money to offer and even if I did, I would not embarrass him or myself so I just thanked him over and over again.

I asked him to take me back to the hotel so we got in his automobile which looked like a bug—it was small but comfortable. He said he would call the hotel the next day. When I got to my room, I tiptoed to my bed.

I thought I would tell them all about it the next day but nobody asked me a thing, they gave me the silent treatment. As I thought about the previous night, I wondered why this guy didn't take me in his arms and try to make love to me. Oh well, I guess I wasn't his type.

Judy finally came around and wanted me to tell her all about my adventure. She said, "From now on, you don't go anywhere without me. I want to share in the fun you're having." She said, "Dottie, we're going to have lunch at a sidewalk café today. I enjoy that and if any reporters come up to talk to us, keep your mouth shut."

A few hours later, Judy and I were having lunch in a cafe. We were plainly dressed and nobody even noticed us. Judy wore sunglasses but I didn't. I noticed that Judy's voice sounded peculiar as she sat there. She was in a strange mood and said, "What would happen to me if I lost my voice?"

"Well, you'd use your hands as you always do so stop this chit-chat, nothing is going to happen to your voice. You know, in the Bible it is written, 'My cup runneth over.' Your cup will be running over long after you're gone because your public will never let you die. Now let's get you out of this foul mood you're in or I'll give you something to worry about. I'll order a big glass of wine and you know what that will do to me!"

That night, we did a little packing and we were back to London. The crowds were waiting for Judy as usual. After finishing our last performance, we were headed back to the States and the grim news we were about to give Minnelli. Vincente knew that Sid was traveling all over Europe with Judy. And I don't think he really cared that much because he was pretty well fed up by now.

Judy's marriage to Vincente had run its course and Judy was starting a whole new adventure. I thought I'd be right there with her every step but it didn't turn out that way. Not long after we got back to California, I started getting some really bad symptoms. It took a while but I was finally diagnosed with multiple sclerosis. It was a bad break but what are you going to do?

6.

House of Memories

My mind and heart are so full of these wonderful people. I can sense them in every room in my house. That's why I am never lonesome. I have laughed and cried with them and there was never a dull moment. My friends in the business would tell me the deepest secrets in their hearts whether they were good or bad. That was true for the men stars as well as the women. Somehow they looked at me as some kind of good witch so they could pour their hearts out to me.

My house is a house of memories wherever you look; or whenever you see some of the beautiful things they have brought into my home. Sometimes, when I lie in bed at night, I think of the things that Judy, Marlene, Joan, and the others have told me. I become hysterical from laughing, I know they're going to put me in a straight-jacket but I love all of my memories and I love all of the people who made them.

My house was a happy house. If it had arms, it would put them around me and say, "Welcome home, Dottie," because my house loved me and I loved it.

Not that every memory was so rosy. I remember a night a long time ago, as I opened the front door, the gas fumes almost knocked me to the ground. I ran through the house to see where it was coming from. I saw that someone had tampered with the oven. I turned off the gas and opened up all the windows. I ran through my house to the master bedroom and found Mike Todd and Joan Blondell making whoopee in my bed.

I screamed at them and said, "Do you realize you could have killed yourself and blown up my house at the same time?" They told me the house was so cold so they lit the oven but didn't wait to see it light up!

When I wasn't over at Judy's house, I used to love to come home and cook a nice big New England dinner. I'd bake a nice apple pie, too, as cooking was my hobby whenever I got a chance to do it. I remember the time Joan Blondell called from New York. She was giving a party and wanted to know how I made my famous deep dish apple pie.

She said, "How do I do it, Dot? I want it to come out just like yours." I told her to make her pie crust on the bottom of the pan a little thicker. Then slice her apples kind of thick and fill her pan with these sliced apples. Then mix some brown sugar with ground walnuts and puffed raisins and pour it over the apples very thin. Add some more apples and repeat this, don't forget to put little pieces of butter with it before you add the top layer of dough. Let your pie get nice and light brown, then slice cheese over the top and put it back in the oven. Watch it closely so the cheese doesn't burn. Serve it with sour cream or whatever you like best.

That wasn't the only time Joan called me about baking all the way from New York. Those calls must have cost her a pretty penny. She also made me walk her through my lemon cheesecake. I poured a lot of love into my baking and cooking, that's why it always came out so good.

My house was like a halfway house during those years. If people couldn't get in through the door or the windows, they would come down through the chimney. One evening, when I got home from work, I noticed a light. I said, "Uh-oh, somebody must be in there." The radio was on, the music was playing, and there was Judy sitting on the den floor. I said, "How did you get in?"

She said, "I heard you telling someone there was a key under the mat."

I said, "Okay, come on in the kitchen, we'll fix something to eat," but Judy wouldn't budge off the floor. When she got up, I could smell the liquor that she had spilled all over her pants, and my new rug was stained but good. I got her into a pair of my slacks and the only damage done was to the rug on my den floor.

Shortly after that, Vincente Minnelli drove up to the house and rang the bell. He asked, "How would you kids like to see Kay Thompson and the Williams Brothers?" Andy Williams and his three brothers were opening that night at Ciro's.

Judy said, "Okay, but only if you take us to La Rue's for dinner first," since La Rue's had the best food in town and we thought the food at Ciro's was lousy. Judy and I got dressed up like Astor's pet horse because everybody and his uncle would be at this opening.

At La Rue's, as we started to order our dinner, Vincente said, "Let's order some crabs." We did, and as I was eating it, these great big strawberries began to break out on my face, one after the other. Judy laughed so loud and drew so much attention that everybody wanted to know what was going on at our table.

Judy said, "Look, this is magic, here comes another one!" meaning another strawberry. I had about ten fat strawberries on my face.

Spencer Tracy walked over to the table and said, "What's all the hilarity?" and Judy said, "Look at Dottie's face, she is breaking out like she has smallpox."

By that time, I was getting a little frightened but Spencer said,

"It must be something she's allergic to. It's probably the crabmeat." They took the crabmeat away and brought me towels full of ice. The swelling went down and within two hours, I looked almost normal again.

Ciro's was packed that night, because everybody in the industry was there. Kay Thompson danced like she was a gazelle and the Williams Brothers were great. I knew Kay very well. She came over to the table and said, "Dottie, who hit you in the face with a tomato?"

Judy said, "You should have seen her two hours ago. It wasn't tomatoes, it was strawberries!"

Oh, we had such wonderful times during those years, so many happy times in my little house and in this city I love so much.

I miss the rings of the telephone during the night, at two, three, or four in the morning. That's when Judy would be walking up and down from one room to another and would call me and say, "Are you asleep Dottie?" I used to wish I could get a good night's sleep, but what could you do with Judy—you just had to talk to her. I never regret what I went through with Judy and I would do it all over again, hitting the high spots and low spots of her life, her marriages and her babies, her opening nights, the cries and laughter that came from her, and how she shared this home of mine.

I remember all of our great times at the studio with Judy and the others—talking to people who were in my make-up chair, on the sets of these wonderful pictures, in their dressing rooms, or at the commissary. The commissary was like a playground for grown-ups, It was filled with superstars who sometimes seemed like a bunch of kids in a kindergarten. I saw Walter Pidgeon and Clark Gable start boxing, and Gary Grant at another table playing jokes with Franchot Tone. Ethel Barrymore would yell at everyone to sit down and behave themselves and stop acting like a bunch of children.

Jack Benny and Joan Blondell visiting Judy and Dottie in the MGM commissary.

Stars from other studios would drive over to MGM just for laughs. I remember when Joan Blondell, Judy, and I were having lunch and Jack Benny came over to the table and said, "I've got a couple of new jokes I want to try out on you girls." Well, the reaction he got from us satisfied him and he said. "Alright kids, this lunch is on me. "

Gee, I'm getting tired now, this goddamn MS is starting to work on me. I better hit the hay as I can go on with this book until I get to be a hundred, but I've got to stop somewhere as I know Judy is telling me to finish the book and get up here. So, you see, there is nothing to fear, as the old saying goes, but fear itself, and I have a sneaking feeling that I am going to have a ball with the bunch that's up there waiting for me.

I loved the life I led. It was exciting and full of fun, and every moment of my life meant something to me. I always tried to help the other guy, so why did I have to get this sickness that slowly kills you and nobody can help you? Well, some day, when I'm pushing up daisies, they'll find a cure and even though I won't be here, I'll be thankful for the other guys.

So laugh and be merry as long as you can. I think I will close as I have a long journey ahead of me, without any fears or regrets. Well, I'm going to stop right now as I need to take it easy and be ready for what comes next.

Que sera sera,

Dottie

Epilogue

by Meredith Ponedel

It was in the summer of 1959 that my father, brother, and I moved into my Aunt Dot's house just inside the border of Beverly Hills—"the flats" as they were called. My mother had died suddenly, leaving me confused, frightened, and lonely. All of a sudden I was uprooted from all that I had known—a familiar house, a grandmother, and several pets I loved dearly. Dot's house seemed dark and dingy in comparison and worst of all for me, there were no animals. My aunt couldn't have any in her house.

Although we had visited Dot from time to time, she was basically a stranger to me. She was 61 at that time, and had been diagnosed with multiple sclerosis several years earlier. From my three-year-old point of view, she was ancient. I was suspicious of the walker she needed to help her get around. I just didn't understand who she was or why she was suddenly a major part of my life.

Enter Judy.

During some of my early explorations of the house, I had come across a bunch of records packed away in a box. Since my father, Bernard "Beans" Ponedel, Dot's younger brother, worked as a make-up man for Frank Sinatra, I was used to seeing a lot of records around, most with Frank's face on the cover. But the lady on the cover of these records in my aunt's house was not at all familiar to me. I liked her right off the bat. With her dark coloring and pretty face, she reminded me of my mother. I already knew how to operate the Webcor record player that had been my mother's—one of the few things of hers that we had taken with us when we moved into my aunt's house.

Without asking permission, I took the records out of the box, back to my room, and put them on to play. I liked what I heard. I didn't understand the songs, but immediately connected to the warmheartedness of her tones, the kindness inherent in the timbre of her voice. I recognized one song immediately and was very happy to hear it: "Over the Rainbow." My mother had sung it to me many times. That this lady knew the same song was just amazing to me. I felt a little less abandoned, finding this touch of home and my mother.

Records were a big part of my life as a young child. I had the collection of my mother's 45s along with a number of children's stories on 78 records. Most of these records came in sets with accompanying picture books—the written story and pictures along with the record and at various intervals, the listener was instructed to "turn the page" in order to continue the story. My favorites were the "Bozo" records. I was totally convinced that the character of Bozo, and the others that I listened to, actually lived within the tiny scroll marks on the vinyl disk. When I was listening to my records, I was oblivious of anything else going on around me.

One day, I was lost in record land when Dot received a visitor. Usually, when Dot had company, I'd go investigate to see if it was anyone interesting. But this time, I was very comfortably ensconced on the floor and I didn't want to leave my music. Dimly, I heard Dottie's walker squeaking down the hallway. The next thing I knew, Dot had brought a lady to my bedroom door.

"Meredith, this is Judy."

I looked up to see a woman with short, dark hair, almost the color of my mother's. She smiled down at me. I liked her smile and smiled back. Dot continued, "This is the lady who sings on your record," pointing to one of the record covers scattered on the floor in front of me. I looked at the cover, which showed a pretty, dark-haired lady with her hair done nicely. I looked at Judy, who had no make-up on and whose hair was—well, it wasn't "done"—and I balked. No way could this big, grown-up person fit into the teeny tiny grooves on those records! No way did she look like the glamorous woman on the record cover. I gave her a good look up and down and came to my own conclusion.

"Nope," I stated flatly, looking up at this stranger. "That's not you." A big grin spread across Judy's face as a great guffaw escaped her lips. Dot was incredulous.

"What do you mean that's not her? I just told you it is!"

Well, I was a hard nut to crack, even at that tender age, and I wasn't buying any of it, grown-ups or not. I looked up at the suspect again and confirmed my suspicions. Nope, this was definitely not the same lady.

I looked at Judy, who, still grinning, had crouched down so she was at eye level with me and got the strange feeling that this was no ordinary "grown-up" I was dealing with. I felt a big smile creep across my face. She might not be the lady in my record, but I liked her anyway!

She was certainly different, this particular friend of Dot's. Now, Dot had a lot of visitors; people were always streaming through the house and I never knew who I'd see when I woke up in the morning or who might pay a midnight (or later) visit.

I enjoyed spending time with all of Dot's old friends who would come to visit. Gail Patrick was very much "the lady" and often brought me boxes of clothes including stiff petticoats and that horrible lace underwear that little girls used to wear that I hated. Frances Dee would enthrall me with her stories of living on a ranch—and being married to a real cowboy! Of course, the "cowboy" was actor Joel McCrea, but I didn't know that. I only knew that she was always telling Dot to have my dad bring me out to "the country" so I could visit her.

But I especially loved it when Judy and Joan Blondell came over. Joan was practically part of the furniture. She'd come over and take me with her to do the shopping for Dot. I spent so much time with Joan, either at my house or hers, that I accepted her as just another relative. I adored Joan Blondell. She was warm, friendly, outgoing, and gave great hugs! She also had another claim to fame—a big one, as far as I was concerned. She had two Pug dogs, Bridey and Freshey. "The Girls," as they were known to all who knew Joan, were as much a part of her as if they were extra limbs.

Dot's house, having been built in the 1930s, had a rather large kitchen with many cabinets, but the cabinet next to the refrigerator (or "ice box" as Dot called it) was the only one without handles and therefore, there was no way of opening it—or at least, that's what my five-year-old self thought.

The mystery of this cabinet led to all sorts of speculation on my part and, with my vivid imagination, I finally hit upon the reason as to why it could not be opened: There was a dead baby inside! When I told Dot what I thought was my perfectly rational explanation, she just laughed it off—as did almost every other adult who heard my theory. A natural reaction of most adults to an over-imaginative child, right?

One day, one of those adults visiting was Judy Garland. As luck would have it, we were all in the kitchen preparing to have ice cream and Dot had special dishes for this treat in a cabinet too high up for me to reach so, as Judy was getting the dishes out, I decided she, too, needed to know about the horrible secret hiding in the cabinet with no handles.

"Do you know why you can't open that door? Do you know what's in there?" I asked her, while pointing to the offending door. Judy looked at the cabinet and then looked at me with a questioning look. "There's a dead baby in there!" I triumphantly announced, totally expecting the usual response of "Oh no there isn't, don't be silly."

That wasn't the response I got.

"I know," said Judy solemnly, getting down on my level to drive home the point. "And her name is Mergatroyd!" I was so shocked at her response I was speechless. My mouth dropped open and I let out a yell of terror. Here was a grown-up agreeing with me—there WAS a dead baby in there! I was horrified. I didn't know what do or what to say. I was frozen. I looked over at Dot who had started to laugh—and chastise me and Judy at the same time.

"Oh for God's sake, there's no dead baby in there—the two of you are impossible!" With that, Dot leaned over, pressed a specific spot on the door and it sprang open, revealing nothing more sinister than glassware. I was kind of sorry to see Mergatroyd go.

As a kid, I never understood that people like Judy Garland and Joan Blondell were "Big Stars," they were just my aunt's friends and I loved being with them. I used to get very excited when I'd come home to see Joan's fire engine red station wagon parked out in front.

I especially liked going to Canter's Deli with Joan because I didn't have to behave the way I did if I was with my dad or my grandmother. Joan let me have a lot more fun than they did. Sometimes, she'd bring her daughter, Ellen, with her to our house and while Dot and Joan would talk in the kitchen, Ellen and I would stay in the yard and visit. Ellen was quite a bit older than I was but she, like her mother, was very fun to be with. Unlike a lot of teenagers who didn't have the patience to bother with children, Ellen had a great deal of tolerance and would talk to me like I was one of her own friends.

Dot felt bad that she couldn't attend my 8th grade graduation because of her illness so she asked Joan to go in her place. Joan came over that afternoon and sat outside with Dot while I was in the bathroom getting ready. I remember that I wanted to wear make-up and already knew how to properly apply it but wanted either Dot or Dad to do it. Dot said no, that I should do it myself and Joan agreed with her. I did my make-up in stages and came out often to have Joan and Dot inspect me and give me tips. When I was finally done, I apparently not only passed inspection but, as I was going back in the house, I heard Joan tell Dot it looked like she and Dad weren't the only make-up artists in the family. I was thrilled.

During the graduation ceremony, I could see Joan in the audience, along with my father and grandmother, but for whatever reason, it was Joan I was focused on. Her face just stood out. She was really beaming.

The next day, I went back to school to help the teachers and I was practically mobbed by my teachers all asking me about Joan! I was amazed. They were very impressed that she was there and I had no idea why. A few of them mentioned some movies she had been in so when I went home I asked Dot if she knew that Joan had been a movie star! I had no idea. As with Judy, what Joan did was never played up. She was just Joan.

Later on, when Joan was in the TV series *Here Come the Brides*, she'd tell Dad to bring me to the set to visit. By then, I had a better grasp of who she was. I'd have a blast visiting the set. I'd get the full VIP treatment from everyone once it was known I was not only "Beans" Ponedel's kid but a special guest of Joan's. I'd sit with Joan in her dressing room between scenes. She'd receive visitors, either guest stars from that particular week or some of the regulars. Sooner or later, everyone ended up in her dressing room and it was a wonderful party. I loved every second of it.

Joan only got mad at me once that I remember. I had just had a fight with Dot about something. I was really mad so I stupidly said something bad about Dot in front of Joan. Boy, did I get it! Joan was furious—I'd never seen her so upset! Her beautiful crystal blue eyes turned ice blue and she let me have it. I was told, in no uncertain terms, that I didn't dare speak against Dot the way I had. A lot of it was the usual spiel about all that Dot had done for me and how she felt bad for my father who had no place to go after my mother died and how I should be grateful that I lived the way I did and all that kind of thing. She was so mad I wondered if she'd ever like me again. But once it was over, it was over, almost as though it had never happened. Joan was great that way. I learned my lesson that it was not okay to insult Dot to her best buddy. I should have known better because I had done almost the exact same thing a few years earlier—with Judy!

I had also had some kind of argument with Dot and had trounced off to my room. Judy came over a short while later and came in to see me. Still furious, I said something along the lines of wishing that Dot were dead. That didn't go over too well, to say the least. Unlike Joan, who seemed to grow bigger as she got angry, Judy sort of condensed. She didn't say anything right away, her eyes didn't get big or change color—but they changed, somehow. She suddenly looked totally different—very intense and I knew that I was in big trouble.

Judy got very quiet and just looked at me. I wanted to run away but I didn't dare. When she did speak, her voice was very cold—if I had been standing in front of the refrigerator, I couldn't have felt any colder. She asked me how I could have dared say something like that about Dot after all she had done for me. She also said something about how I should learn to appreciate what I had instead of always complaining about what I didn't have.

Arguing with Dot was bad enough—I couldn't handle arguing

with Judy, too. Unlike the incident with Joan, it wasn't over right away. Judy left me in my room but I could feel her angry energy around me. It was almost as though it was still in the house even when she left. Unlike many adults, though, who forced kids to apologize for something they had done, neither Joan nor Judy asked that of me or even mentioned it. Maybe they thought I should figure that one out on my own. And I did.

I think I was about eight years old when Judy first asked me if I wanted to go to England with her. She said she was bringing her kids, Lorna and Joe, with her and wondered if I would like to come, too. Would I? Wow! I remember running to Dot and yelling the whole way that Judy wanted me to go with her to England.

"What's all this about?" asked Dot. She spoke to Judy for a while as I hovered around, anxious for an answer. Dot's answer was a typical, "We'll see." I couldn't understand why she just didn't say yes immediately. I was so excited at the thought of going with Judy—what fun we'd have! Just the idea of being there with her and her kids excited me beyond belief, I wanted to go so badly. Dot said she'd have to discuss it with Daddy. Ugh. Why couldn't she just say yes?

As usual, Daddy was ambivalent and Dot said she didn't think it was a good idea. Dot knew how headstrong and adventurous I could be and didn't think Judy would be able to handle me. I heard her say that she was afraid Judy would lose me if I decided to go exploring on my own. "Judy won't lose me! I promise!" I blurted out, but I couldn't change Dot's mind.

A few days later, after much arguing and pleading, I had to tell Judy that I couldn't go. I was heartbroken. I'll never forget her voice on the other end of the phone. She sounded as disappointed as I was. But she accepted Dot's verdict. When I heard how sad she sounded, I got really mad. I hated it when Judy was sad and this time it was Dot's fault! I told Judy how mad I was at Dot and how

I was going to keep trying to get her to let me go. I was surprised at Judy's reaction. "No," she said, quietly but firmly. "When Dottie says no, it's no. No use to keep trying. Just leave it alone." I knew she was right but I was still touched that Judy was disappointed I couldn't go with them.

It was a tradition at our house to watch Judy's TV show that was on CBS in the early 1960s every Sunday night. While on some level I was aware that she was a public figure, I was still very young and part of me thought her show was private—just for us.

Each week, right after Judy's TV show ended, she'd call Dot and the two of them would talk about the show. Sometimes Dad would chime in, too, with his opinions. So it was pretty much standard that when the phone would ring a few minutes after her show ended, I would answer it and Judy would ask me how I liked the show. I'd tell her what I liked and what I didn't like. Dot always told me to remember to tell Judy that she looked beautiful.

Dot and Dad, however, had the privilege of being a bit more critical. I remember once when Dad really had it in for whoever had done her make-up that week. "Who the hell did you?" he yelled in the general direction of the phone as Dot took it from me. "He made you look like a raccoon!" So much for Daddy's constructive criticism.

One Sunday night in particular, we settled in to watch her show. I was in Daddy's room watching on his TV while Dot watched from her bed in her own room, as usual. Toward the end of the show, during the trunk scene while she was singing, she looked into her trunk and pulled out a puppy! I was ecstatic since I immediately assumed the puppy was for me. Everyone who knew me knew that the one thing I wanted most was a puppy. Dot and Dad knew how badly I wanted one but since Dot couldn't get around easily and Daddy was away at work all the time, it was just not practical to have a pet. They had each had dogs before and they both loved animals; and for this reason they knew the kind of work having a dog entailed and knew I wasn't up to it at that age. Judy certainly knew that I wanted a dog; as with everyone else who visited, I had asked her for one, so when I saw her take that puppy out of the drawer in the trunk, I just flipped.

"She got me a puppy!" I screamed at the top of my lungs. "Dottie, Dottie, she got me a puppy!" I ran into Dot's room practically vaulting over her walker in the doorway and jumped up and down in front of her as though I were on fire. "It's mine, it's mine, it's mine!"

Dad had followed me into her room in an effort to calm me down. "It's not yours," they both said at the same time. Dot, who apparently knew what was going to happen, told me to quiet down and watch Judy's next move. She finished the song, took the puppy to the end of the stage, and handed it to her young son, Joey, who was sitting there.

And all hell broke loose in Beverly Hills!

"Noooooooo!" I wailed at the top of my lungs! "That's my puppy!" Running out of Dot's room and dodging my father's grasp, I ran into my room and proceeded to have a huge temper tantrum. I was prone to having them anyway but this one was a real doozy. Dolls were swept off the beds onto the floor. I overturned the large table in the center of my room and all the books spilled out of the drawers. The spreads came off the beds and I opened the drawers in the two end tables and threw everything out.

As I raged, Dot and Dad just stayed out of my way. I was so angry at Judy for what I saw as her complete betrayal that I couldn't stand it. I was still raging when the phone rang. I stopped and stood still for a moment, knowing darn well who was on the other end.

"Meredith, get the phone!" Dot called out to me. She knew who was calling, too, and wanted me to get control over myself. I stood in the doorway of my destroyed room and looked down the hall at

Dot. The phone, which was sitting on the brown leather seat of her walker, was still ringing.

"No!" I responded angrily. "I hate her and I never want to talk to her again!" I stormed back into my bedroom and fumed. The phone stopped ringing. A minute later, it started ringing again. Again Dot called out to me.

"Meredith, you better answer it. Judy's going to wonder what's wrong if we don't answer."

"I don't care," I was adamant. Again the phone stopped ringing. This time, no one said anything.

About two or three minutes went by and the phone rang again. This time Dad called out from his room, "Will someone answer the damn phone? She's going to send the police out here soon if she doesn't get an answer!" He was probably right. Judy knew that Dot would only leave the house in an emergency and very likely would have called the police if the phone weren't answered soon.

Dot picked up the receiver, not even bothering to say hello. "You are in big trouble," I heard her say. I moved off my bed and stood closer to the doorway so I could hear—in spite of myself. There was quiet for a minute while Dot listened. Then she laughed. I heard her describe the events of the past 20 minutes to Judy. However, she did it in such a way as to place the blame on Judy. "What the heck did you hand that puppy to Joey for?" She asked. "You know how much Meredith wants a puppy." At that, I came out of my room and stood in the hall. Dot looked over at me and winked.

"Now Judy," she admonished her. "That wasn't a very nice thing to do." This was more like it, as far as I was concerned. After all, the whole thing was Judy's fault. I slowly inched my way down the hall as Dot placed the blame squarely where it belonged. I caved. But even in my anger, which was now rapidly dissipating, I was fully aware that Judy was too special to deserve this kind of treatment.

"Don't yell at Judy, Dottie," I said. "It wasn't all her fault." I had made my way into her room and was standing by her bed.

Dot looked up, eyes wide with mock astonishment. "It's not all Judy's fault?" she said, half to me and half into the receiver. I stood there quietly, not yet willing to fully admit my guilt. I could hear Judy saying something through the receiver and Dot listened for a moment and then held the phone out to me.

"Judy wants to tell you about her 17 dogs and 14 cats."

"WHAT?!" Now it was my turn to be astonished. "Judy has 17 dogs and 14 cats?" This was news to me. Dot had a big grin on her face as I spoke into the phone.

"Do you really have 17 dogs and 14 cats?"

"Yes, I do," came the reply from a voice I knew and loved and couldn't possibly stay angry with. "And you can come over and play with them anytime you want."

"Wow! Dottie! Judy says I can go and play with her dogs and cats whenever I want!" I was happy again, the previous upset had gone totally out of my head. I had bought Judy's tale—hook, line, and sinker. On cloud nine, I handed the phone back to Dot and told her to make sure Judy knew that I was only too willing to help her clean up after her animals. I knew that was an important part of having animals and I wanted to make sure they were taken care of.

As I turned to go back to my room, I heard Dot say rather quietly into the phone, "Now what are you going to do if she comes over?"

I remember the very last conversation I had with Judy. She had been calling a lot very late at night to talk to Dot. I knew that Judy had been talking to my aunt about some big money worries she was having. I remember asking Dot after one of these calls why she just didn't help Judy out by giving her money. Dot certainly wasn't wealthy, she didn't have the kind of money it would have taken to pay off Judy's debts, but I thought she could have done something for her.

Dot would explain to me that she didn't give Judy money because if she had, Judy wouldn't have used it wisely and would still have ended up in trouble. I didn't fully understand any of this at the time. I was old enough by then to have my own opinions on things and I felt very bad for Judy. It was hard to hear the phone calls night after night and hear Dot say no to her. I would argue with Dot that someone should help Judy and Dot would always say that the best someone to help Judy was Judy but that Judy didn't see it that way.

So, I came up with my own plan. I had saved up a little money, about $100 or so, and I wanted to give it to Judy. Of course, I had no idea just how much money she really needed. I was often asleep when Judy would call and the ringing would wake me up. I decided to force myself to stay awake one night so I could grab the phone before Dot heard it. The phone was always placed on the seat of Dot's wheelchair so that she could grab it in case of emergency. During the day, it was in its place in the booth in the wall.

The cord wasn't quite long enough to stretch all the way to my room—almost, but not quite. So one night when I was determined to stay awake, I waited until Dot was asleep and very carefully took the phone and put it on the floor by my door. And waited. I sat up on the floor with my back to the doorway which was very uncomfortable so I figured that would keep me awake. It did. It was really important that I answered the phone on the first ring because Dot had ears like a bat and could hear someone whispering a mile away. Somehow, I stayed awake and sure enough, at around two in the morning, the phone rang. I snatched the receiver off the hook even before the first ring had finished. Judy was really surprised to hear my voice. I didn't even say hello, just, "Judy?"

"Meredith, is that you? What are you doing up? Let me speak to Dottie."

It was now or never and I took the plunge. "Judy, I have something for you. I have a hundred dollars saved up and I want to give it to you."

Silence. Then she repeated what she had said before without acknowledging what I had said. "Let me speak with Dottie!"

"But Judy—" I started to say and was interrupted.

Very quietly, she said, "I heard you—now let me speak to Dottie." That was it. There was a finality to her voice and I knew I couldn't get any further with her. I had no idea why she hadn't been more receptive to my offer and I felt as though I had failed her. I thought I had the answer and that I was doing Judy a favor by offering her something she wanted. I slowly got to my feet, as I picked up the phone to take it to Dot, I saw that she was awake and had heard the entire exchange. She gave me a very strange look as I handed her the phone. I started to cry and I went back to my room. That was the last time I remember speaking with Judy.

Dot called me into her room the next morning—which was kind of unusual because she was usually up before me. "So what you wanted to do didn't work, did it?" She didn't seem surprised that it hadn't. I still was very confused and I told her that all I wanted to do was to help Judy because it seemed like no one else wanted to help her.

"Do you think I don't want to help Judy, is that what you think?" She wasn't angry when she said it, just kind of sad. I hung my head, not knowing what to say. Of course I knew that Dot loved Judy, I just didn't know why she wouldn't do what Judy asked and I said so.

What she said next confused me even more. "Nobody can help Judy, Meredith, nobody." I could tell that this wasn't easy for Dot to say and she was choosing her words very carefully. "Judy has to help herself, and she just won't do it. Do you think I haven't wanted to? Do you think I like seeing her this way? I've been telling her that for years and so have a lot of other people. Judy doesn't want to see what she doesn't want to see and no one can change that. When she calls here, it's not about the money. It's never really about the money." She looked at me very directly. "You did not fail her last night," Dot said very emphatically, as though she had read my mind. How did she know? I was shocked and started to cry again. I still felt terrible about the whole thing.

"Then why does she call?" I asked, not really understanding the subtleties of the situation.

"She calls because she doesn't know what else to do. She brings on these problems herself and then expects everyone else to get her out of them."

I obviously didn't understand and I felt that Dot was being way too hard on Judy. As far as I was concerned, if Judy needed help she should have it. Period. Dot was a firm believer in people helping themselves and she could see I was getting lost in all this. She tried a different approach.

"Meredith, Judy doesn't want to accept responsibility for taking care of herself. Now do you see why I'm always telling you to pay attention to things? To do things for yourself? To follow through?" Dot was right about that—she and Dad were always nagging me about that, especially the "follow through" part, which I couldn't stand.

She went on. "If you don't learn to do these things for yourself now, you never will. Do you want to be making phone calls like this when you're older? Do you think Judy *likes* doing things like this? Judy doesn't like a lot of the things that she does, but she does them anyway."

I think that at one point in time, Dot had been better able to cope with situations like these when they came up but she had just gotten to the point where she was wearing out. These dealings with Judy seemed to be too much for her. Maybe it was her age or the progression of the M.S.—by this time she was in a wheelchair and needed constant help.

At some point around the Christmas I turned 13, Dot was in touch with Judy. After the holiday, Dot asked me how I would feel about spending some of my upcoming summer break with Judy in London. Judy had asked Dot about it and Dot said she would ask me. Needless to say, I was all for it!

As the months went by, Dot started telling me that Judy hadn't been feeling well and she thought it might help to have me around for a while in the summer. This excited me to no end. As time went on, I was very aware that Dot was getting more and more phone calls from various people, including Joan, and they all wanted to talk about Judy. Dot never told me the content of these calls but from what I could glean, something wasn't right. Occasionally, she'd mention that Judy wasn't doing well and that she might need me to help her. That was fine by me. Little by little, Dot would drop hints about how Judy was having problems, how she wasn't exactly the same as she was the last time I had seen her.

As we got closer to summer, I remember Dot and Dad both trying to educate me about English money and the exchange rate. Dad had some English coins and bills and would show me the different denominations and explain how it all worked—all of which went right over my head. Dot also told me about the American Embassy and wanted me to know that I could go there if there was any kind of trouble. She also taught me about making long-distance phone calls and that I shouldn't hesitate to call home collect if necessary.

What I didn't realize then was that Dot was trying to prepare me for what I'd see—how different Judy would be from what she had been like just a few years before. I think the fact that Dot had decided to send me said a lot about how worried she was about Judy. I remember hearing one news report about Judy having a hard time with an audience, that they had thrown things at her. I was very shocked and angry about that.

I think Dot was really torn at that point. She wanted to let me go, at the same time knowing I wasn't prepared for it. I don't really know how much she actually intended for me to go to England to be with Judy that summer. She was torn between wanting to help Judy (knowing that I would have done anything for her) and wanting to protect me at the same time.

Back then, of course, I couldn't understand it. I later came to realize what a quandary it must have been for her. She couldn't take care of Judy and protect me at the same time. I hate to think that she sacrificed Judy for me. Of course, I probably couldn't have saved Judy, but I sure like to think I could have made a difference.

Anyway, the closer it got to June, the more intense things seemed to get. At some point, we saw news reports of Judy's latest marriage and that caused quite a few heated discussions between Dot and Dad. I was still excited about the trip and figured that Judy and I would run around together and have a great time, just as before. I knew that she wasn't feeling well but it wasn't sinking in just how sick she was. Dot knew and she was carefully trying to tell me without scaring me or changing my feelings toward Judy.

As summer approached, I was anxious to leave. I had never traveled, I had never been on a plane, and I was really looking forward to it. I wanted to leave early and not wait until the end of school but Dot kept saying I had to finish.

Then came that day in June when we were all outside. Daddy had his Zenith transistor radio tuned to a news station. Dot was doing some pruning on the roses from her wheelchair. The phone rang and I ran in the house to answer it. It was Joan Blondell and she sounded strange. When I yelled to Dot that Joan was on the phone, she told me to tell her she'd call back later. I could tell Joan wasn't happy about that but she said okay and hung up.

The phone rang a few minutes later. It was Joan again and this time she sounded really bad, as though she was crying, and she insisted that I get Dot right away. So I wheeled Dot up the ramp, through the back porch, and into the kitchen, and I went back outside to Dad. I could hear Dot pick up the receiver and say, "Joan, I was outside—what's going on?"

At that moment, there was a signal on the radio and an announcer broke into the regular news broadcast announcing that Judy Garland had died. Dot, Dad, and I all screamed at the same time and I suddenly knew why Joan had called.

With tears streaming down my face, I ran into the house to find Dot bent over the kitchen table, sobbing, still holding the receiver. I was heartbroken, horrified, and angry. I was angry at Dot for not letting me go to London in time to be with Judy. I was screaming at her as she sobbed, screaming that it was all her fault—if only she had let me go, if only she had given Judy money when she needed it, if only she had let her stay with us, then none of these bad things would have happened. As Dot sobbed helplessly, still holding the phone, I could hear Joan crying on the other end.

The rest of the afternoon passed in a blur. There were lots of phone calls and a parade of people coming to the house to see Dot and cry with her, including Joan. I just sat in my room, numb. I felt as though my whole world had crumbled; that a great light had gone out of the world. I just couldn't believe I'd never see Judy again, never hear the two of them laughing over some story or other, never be part of the shenanigans that Judy could so easily stir up.

I desperately needed to hear Judy's voice. Later that day, I took my record player outside on the front lawn where I liked to sit and feed the birds. It was quiet and peaceful. I got a couple of extension cords and plugged in the record player and just sat on the grass, listening to Judy's records as the sun went down. I thought of Judy's kids, Joey in particular since we were the same age. I was wondering how the world could possibly get along without her when I suddenly heard the squeak of Dot's wheelchair coming from the house. She rolled down to the lawn and stopped her chair, put the brake on, and just sat. She didn't say a word to me—she didn't have to. I knew my anger had been wrong. Deep down I knew it wasn't Dot's fault—and she knew that I knew. We just sat there together, listening to Judy sing as the sun went down.

We went on, of course. The world didn't end as I had thought it might—and as Dot knew it wouldn't. She had been there before, with different people and different relationships. That summer passed, slowly and quietly. I made the gradual discovery that Judy had been a lot more than just the funny and loving friend of the family. I was actually astounded to find out, as the summer wore on and various newspaper and magazine articles reported on her career, that she had been a person who was known all over the world, a brilliant actress and singer.

The only other inkling I had of that had occurred when I was about eight or nine and Judy appeared on *The Ed Sullivan Show*. We knew she was going to be on and I had settled down in Dad's room to watch. To my amazement, the minute she walked out onto the stage, the audience stood up and applauded—long and loud. I asked my father what it meant and he told me about standing ovations and that they happened when an audience wanted to acknowledge a great performer. "So why are they standing for Judy?" I asked, perplexed.

"Because of what she's done," came the answer.

"What's she done?" I just wasn't getting it.

My dad chuckled. "She's a great singer!"

"She is?" So much for my showbiz education.

So, all during that summer when article after article came out about Judy's movie career and her spectacular concert performances,

I just couldn't believe that I hadn't known any of this. I started paying more attention to Dot's friends and their own careers. I asked a lot of questions, including many about Dot's own role in the movie industry. And I gradually accumulated more of Judy's recordings, marveling that a voice I had heard so many times in the personal and private setting of my own home was beloved the world over.

Dot went on, too. Not easily. There were many hard days of tears and not as many of laughter that summer. She had her own support group and spent many hours talking and visiting with friends who could share her experiences; friends who had known them both and knew just what Dot had lost. We both missed Judy and were only too aware of a huge hole in our lives.

Dot lived another ten years, until the spring of 1979. She spent much of her time writing her stories down, wanting to set the record straight. Wanting to shoot down all those who wrote about Judy without knowledge and certainly without love. She wanted people to hear the laughter, to see the beauty, to feel the exquisite intensity of a woman who gave and gave until she herself gave out.

But above all, she wanted people to hear Judy's music, to hear the love and the fear and the laughter and the sadness in that phenomenally expressive voice. She wanted people to know Judy as an extremely gifted performer and a warm and loving human being with frailties just like the rest of us. She wanted Judy to have her due and she was determined to get it for her.

I think she did.

Index

175